FLIGHT

PANTHEON BOOKS

NIEUPORT XVII

FLIGHT
A PANORAMA OF AVIATION

BY MELVIN B. ZISFEIN
Deputy Director, National Air and Space Museum, Smithsonian Institution

ILLUSTRATED
BY ROBERT ANDREW PARKER

Library of Congress Cataloging
in Publication Data

Zisfein, Melvin B.
Flight: a panorama of aviation
    SUMMARY: An illustrated
history of flight from early theories to the present time.
    1. Aeronautics—History—
Juvenile literature.
[1. Aeronautics—History]
  I. Parker, Robert Andrew.
  II. Title.
TL547.Z68   79–9462
629.13′009   AACR1

ISBN 0–394–85042–4

ISBN 0–394–94272–8 lib. bdg.

Manufactured in the United
States of America

DESIGNED BY CLINT ANGLIN

CONTENTS

INTRODUCTION

This book grew out of my love for aviation and my respect and admiration for those who advanced human flight from a dream to an everyday occurance. The story of flight is the story of people and machines, of successes and failures, and it is permeated throughout by the human passion to achieve. This book is an introduction to that story.

Giving as much space to illustration as to text, its purpose is to kindle the kind of enthusiasm for the subject and admiration for its practioners that I feel. A book of this size cannot hold every story, salute every achievement, or show every machine. Consequently, I was forced to include some and omit others; my criteria being very personal. I have included what *I* would like to find in an introductory book.

My publisher and I decided that the book should be illustrated by an artist who could give a full visual interpretation of the facts beyond the often reproduced stock photographs. That led us to the noted painter Robert Andrew Parker, who shares my fascination with the subject of aviation. Parker's pictures seek artistic interpretation rather than photographic reality and convey his personal views of the essence and beauty of the machines and the romantic spirit of the people of flight.

So here it is—a highly personal pictorial summary of the story of flight. If this book makes you eager to learn more, then we've done our job.

—M. B. Z.

FLIGHT

1. MYTHS AND LEGENDS

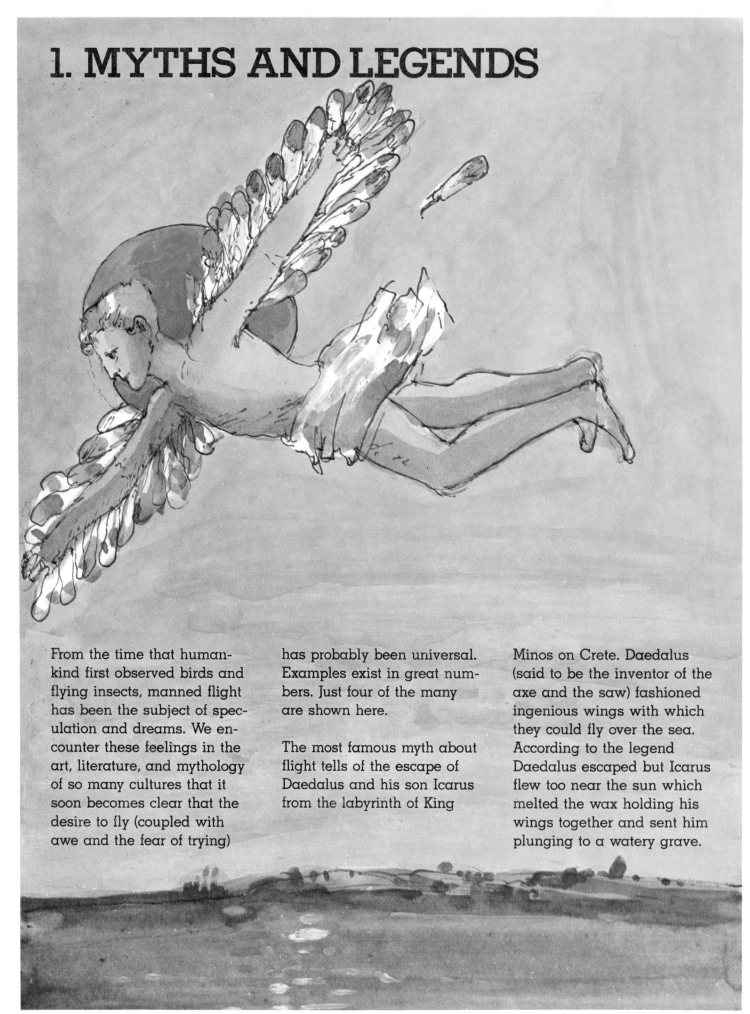

From the time that human-kind first observed birds and flying insects, manned flight has been the subject of speculation and dreams. We encounter these feelings in the art, literature, and mythology of so many cultures that it soon becomes clear that the desire to fly (coupled with awe and the fear of trying) has probably been universal. Examples exist in great numbers. Just four of the many are shown here.

The most famous myth about flight tells of the escape of Daedalus and his son Icarus from the labyrinth of King Minos on Crete. Daedalus (said to be the inventor of the axe and the saw) fashioned ingenious wings with which they could fly over the sea. According to the legend Daedalus escaped but Icarus flew too near the sun which melted the wax holding his wings together and sent him plunging to a watery grave.

ICARUS IN FLIGHT

2

A legend from ancient Persia tells of the King Kai-Kaus who flew on a throne carried aloft by captive eagles.

KING KAI-KAUS

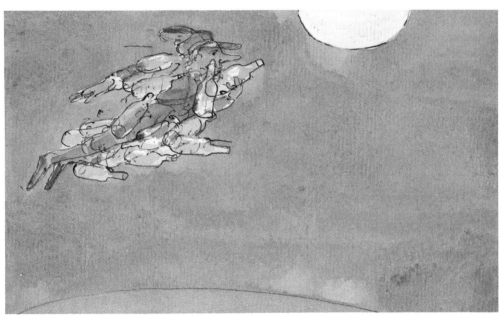

Cyrano de Bergerac, the French poet, wrote of ascending to the Moon by surrounding his body with bottles of dew which lifted him heavenward when rays of the morning sun caused the dew to rise.

CYRANO DE BERGERAC

In a French myth the locksmith Besnier claimed that he flew with the aid of an apparatus driven by his arms and legs. As each of the folded saillike assemblies moved up, it came together to minimize air resistance. On the downstroke, each folded "sail" opened, pushing the structure and rider upward. Besnier's principle bears some resemblance to the way a bird's wingtip feathers drive it through the air.

BESNIER

3

2. BALLOONING

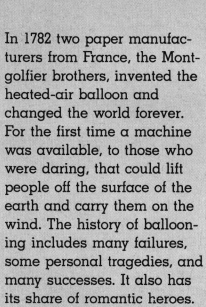

In 1782 two paper manufacturers from France, the Montgolfier brothers, invented the heated-air balloon and changed the world forever. For the first time a machine was available, to those who were daring, that could lift people off the surface of the earth and carry them on the wind. The history of ballooning includes many failures, some personal tragedies, and many successes. It also has its share of romantic heroes.

UNMANNED MONTGOLFIER HEATED-AIR BALLOON

HEATED AIR AND GAS

To make a simple balloon take a light container (like a big nonporous fabric sphere) and fill it with a gas that weighs less than the same volume of air when both are at the same pressure. Hydrogen, helium, heated air, and coal gas are all examples of gasses that can be used to fill a balloon. If the balloon is big enough it can carry additional weights like passengers, cargo, and ballast in a gondola suspended from its underside.

To make a heated-air balloon rise one can heat the air inside (usually by burning some combustible substance in the opening at the bottom of the bag). To make a gas balloon rise one can jettison some ballast weights, carried along for that very purpose. Radiation from the sun also makes a gas balloon rise by heating the gas inside.

To make a heated-air balloon descend one merely stops heating the air inside and allows it to cool. To make a gas balloon descend one lets some of the gas out of the bag, generally by opening a valve at the top. Basically, a balloon is at the mercy of the winds, and to this day a free balloon has the right-of-way over any other flying machine.

MANNED MONTGOLFIER HEATED-AIR BALLOON

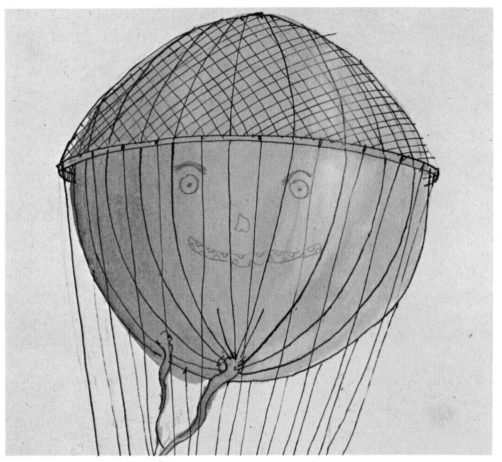

GAS BALLOON

5

THE FIRST MANNED FLIGHT

The Montgolfier brothers, Joseph and Étienne, publicly launched their first heated-air balloon at Annonay, France on June 4, 1783. It was made of cloth lined with paper and carried no passengers.

Then at Versailles on September 19, 1783, before Louis XVI and his court, they sent up a balloon carrying a rooster, a duck, and a sheep in a light cage. The animals, still very much alive after a successful ascent and landing, were proof to all present that it was possible to breathe while in flight.

Finally the Montgolfier brothers were ready for a manned flight. The crew of this first air journey were two aristocratic young gentlemen, the Marquis D'Arlandes and Pilâtre de Rozier. They made a voyage over Paris, on November 21, 1783. The aeronauts bowed and doffed their hats to the people below. They shoveled straw into their fire and extinguished sparks and flames that could have destroyed their huge paper balloon and landed about five miles from their takeoff point after a flight of about twenty-five minutes. Paris went wild!

THE FIRST AERONAUTS

FLIGHT OF THE FIRST HUMAN AERONAUTS: MARQUIS D'ARLANDES AND PILATRE DE ROZIER

The launch in Paris of the Charles unmanned hydrogen balloon was successful, and the little (thirteen-foot diameter) balloon was wafted by the wind about ten miles to the farming village of Gonesse where it burst and fell. The surprised villagers took it for a hideous, evil-smelling monster; they attacked it with pitchforks and "killed it." Then leaving nothing to chance, they tied the remains of the balloon to a horse and dragged it to shreds.

THE FIRST MANNED GAS-BALLOON FLIGHT

Finally, Charles was ready for a manned flight in a big, new hydrogen balloon. He ascended from the Tuilleries Gardens in Paris on December 1, 1783, only ten days after the Montgolfier brothers' flight—too late to be the first person to ascend in a free balloon. Charles took Marie-Noël Robert, one of the builders, with him and they had a fantastically successful two-hour flight to a meadow near Nesle, about twenty-seven miles away. There, Robert left the elegant chariot-shaped gondola and Charles ascended alone to about nine or ten thousand feet. When he landed about thirty-five minutes later, he complained of severe fright, cold, and earaches. Charles, the first gas-balloon aeronaut, had made the world's first two gas-balloon flights in a single day. He then lived another thirty years and never ascended in a balloon again!

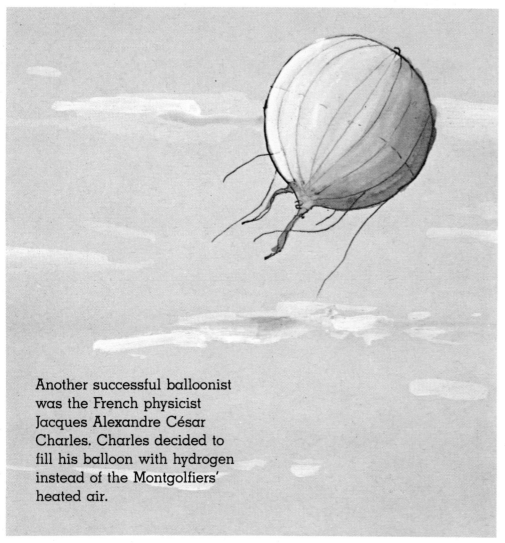

Another successful balloonist was the French physicist Jacques Alexandre César Charles. Charles decided to fill his balloon with hydrogen instead of the Montgolfiers' heated air.

CHARLES UNMANNED HYDROGEN BALLOON

CHARLES BALLOON AFTER LANDING IN GONESSE

FIRST MANNED GAS BALLOON FLIGHT: J.A.C. CHARLES AND M.N. ROBERT

FIRST FLIGHT ACROSS THE ENGLISH CHANNEL: JOHN JEFFRIES AND JEAN-PIERRE BLANCHARD

ACROSS THE ENGLISH CHANNEL

Possibly the most celebrated balloon voyage was also one of the wildest. This was the trip across the English Channel by the American physician John Jeffries and the Frenchman Jean-Pierre Blanchard. Jeffries was a wealthy amateur scientist who put up £700 to finance the project. Blanchard was a professional balloonist. He tolerated Jeffries, but barely.

The gas balloon that Blanchard and Jeffries flew was a fine specimen but it was burdened with all manner of devices that proved to be useless, like aerial oars, a gouvernail or rudder, and a handcranked moulinet or screwtype propeller.

On January 7, 1785, they began their dangerous trip from Dover. The balloon flew well at first and the various fishing vessels they drifted over saluted them. But then, due to inexperienced handling, the balloon began making great arcs in the sky and continued to do so for the remainder of the voyage. The two balloonists were either frantically releasing gas to control too-rapid ascents or even more frantically throwing ballast overboard to keep from falling into the English Channel. At the bottom of the third drop, when it appeared that all was lost and they would plunge into the water, fortune smiled on Blanchard and Jeffries and they unexpectedly ascended over the French coast. They landed safely in the forest of Guines about twelve miles inland from Calais and became the heroes of the day.

JEFFRIES AND BLANCHARD LANDING IN FRANCE

BALLOONS IN WAR

While Benjamin Franklin was the United States envoy to the French court in Paris he witnessed a balloon ascension. When somebody remarked, "What use is it?" Franklin snorted, "What use is a newborn babe?" He then wrote to some of his scientific colleagues showing great interest in the balloon's potential in war.

We have dealt so far with free balloon flights—that is with the flight of balloons which are free to go where the winds take them. In war a captive balloon was sometimes more useful than a free balloon. A captive balloon is kept from drifting by being attached to a rope that is anchored to a ground station. During the Napoleonic Wars two French officers proposed using a captive balloon as a high observation post to report enemy movements. The first use of this balloon was during the Battle of Maubeuge in June 1794. Shortly thereafter the same balloon was used to drop observation reports to the general in command during the Battle of Fleurus. This aerial reconnaissance contributed significantly to the French victory.

MILITARY OBSERVATION BALLOON IN NAPOLEONIC WAR

During the American Civil War balloons were used by both the Union and Confederate armies for reconnaissance. Observations made from balloons during the Battle of Fair Oaks in 1862 were crucial to the Union victory there. The Union forces also placed an observation balloon on board the small vessel *Fanny* and later constructed the first vessel with a flight deck superstructure, the balloon carrier *George Washington Parke Custis.*

BALLON CARRIER *GEORGE WASHINGTON PARKE CUSTIS* IN AMERICAN CIVIL WAR

Possibly the most dramatic use of balloons in war took place in September 1870 during the siege of Paris in the Franco-Prussian War. More than sixty balloons were launched, carrying approximately 160 people and millions of letters out of Paris. These flights originated from the temporarily empty railroad stations and yards.

FRENCH BALLOON CENTER IN FRANCO-PRUSSIAN WAR

The wartime use of balloons has continued into modern times. During World War II the Japanese even turned the balloon into the first intercontinental strategic weapons delivery system. They constructed and launched about 9000 large, hydrogen-filled paper balloons which were designed to cross the Pacific and drop incendiary and fragmentation bombs on the United States. About a thousand fell on target starting numerous fires and killing at least six people. The wartime suppression of all this news seems to have caused the Japanese to believe that their five-month war-balloon program had failed and they gave it up.

JAPANESE WAR BALLOON

BALLOONS TODAY

Modern balloons of both the heated air and gas varieties are still in use for special purposes such as weather and high altitude research, and advertising and sport. Here is a view of a massive launch of heated-air sport balloons.

HEATED-AIR SPORT BALLOONS

13

3. DIRIGIBLES

As soon as ballooning advanced beyond the stunt stage, the search began for a balloon that could be steered: a "dirigible" balloon. A good dirigible balloon requires engines, propellers, and steering mechanisms to control the flight. Its oblong shape was devised to obtain some aerodynamic lift and to minimize air resistance. A dirigible must retain its shape constantly no matter how speed, altitude, or temperature may affect it. The prob-lems of dirigible flight were solved gradually as various inventors improved on what their predecessors had ac-complished.

EARLY DIRIGIBLES

In 1852 Henri Giffard of France built a dirigible bal-loon or airship, as they were also called. It was the first airship that was somewhat controllable when it flew slowly through relatively calm air. Because better en-gines did not exist at that time it had to be powered by a heavy, inefficient steam en-gine.

Beginning in 1898 in Paris, after some more progress had been made by various inventors, a colorful Brazilian named Alberto Santos-Dumont built a series of air-ships which made him fa-mous. His sixth airship won him a coveted prize when he flew it seven miles, from St. Cloud to the Eiffel Tower and back in less than a half hour.

GIFFARD DIRIGIBLE

Here we see Santos-Dumont enjoying some food and drink at a sidewalk café, having tied his latest airship to a nearby lamppost. He would continue in aviation to become in 1906 the first person in Europe to fly an airplane.

SANTOS-DUMONT DIRIGIBLE

15

LZ4 ZEPPELIN

THE ZEPPELINS

The most intensive search for a practical dirigible was made by the German Count Ferdinand von Zeppelin, and the staff that he brought together. Beginning in the 1870s Zeppelin and his associates moved from failure to failure, from disappointment to disappointment, somehow always managing to find new support when it appeared certain that none existed.

They called their dirigibles Zeppelins. The first four were the LZ1, which didn't perform well; the LZ2, which was wrecked in a heavy wind after its power plants failed; the LZ3, which made many successful flights and restored public confidence in Zeppelins; and, in 1908, the LZ4, which flew successfully over the Alps for twelve hours.

Many more Zeppelins were subsequently built. They carried passengers—the first commercial airline service—and later were used as giant and terrifying bombers against England in World War I.

GERMAN ZEPPELIN OVER LONDON, WORLD WAR I

THE *HINDENBURG* OVER NEW YORK CITY

After the war Germany turned some Zeppelins over to Great Britain, France, and the United States, while others were used to reestablish German airline service. Dirigibles were also designed, built, and flown by Great Britain, France, and the United States, some with considerable success, but airships like the LZ127, the famous *Graf Zeppelin*, kept Germany the leader in airship progress.

THE END OF THE ZEPPELINS

One of the last Zeppelins was the LZ129 named for the German Chancelor von Hindenburg. The *Hindenburg* first flew in 1936. Filled with hydrogen she could carry a payload of about 40,000 pounds and cross the Atlantic Ocean with ease.

On May 6, 1937, the *Hindenburg* (recently modified to contain seventy-two passenger berths) was destroyed in a fire while landing at Lakehurst, New Jersey. Public confidence in dirigibles as passenger carriers disappeared and the day of the Zeppelin was over. Actually, airplanes were evolving so rapidly that dirigibles probably wouldn't have lasted for more than a few years as a form of mass transportation, but the *Hindenburg* disaster provided a shocking and dramatic conclusion to a most interesting era of flight.

CRASH OF THE *HINDENBURG*

4. THE DAWN OF THE AIRPLANE

A SIMPLIFIED CONCEPT OF THE AIRPLANE

The concept of the airplane evolved gradually as a result of observations of bird flight, experimentation with gliders and kites, and out of study and reasoning done by scientists, mathematicians, and technologists.

The need for wings was suggested by the observation of birds and insects. Birds and insects have wings which flap to generate lift and also to propel them through the air. However, it became apparent that a flying machine would work much better with non-flapping wings pulled through the air to generate sufficient lifting force to hold up the weight of the machine.

Moreover, non-flapping wings could be made to generate lift using a separate device to propel the wings through the air. This device became known as the propeller. The propeller is actually a twisted wing so contoured that when it is rotated by an engine it produces a force like lift but aimed in a forward direction. This force, known as thrust, pulls the airplane through the air so that its wings can develop lift and hold the airplane up.

Responding to this thrust the airplane would keep going faster and faster if it did not generate another force called drag which opposes the forward motion of the airplane, increasing until a speed is reached at which the drag is equal to the thrust.

By knowing the significance of these terms—lift, weight, thrust, and drag—we can appreciate the most fundamental principle of true flight. An airplane is in level, steady flight when its lift equals its weight and its drag equals its thrust.

INSPIRATION FOR HUMAN FLIGHT

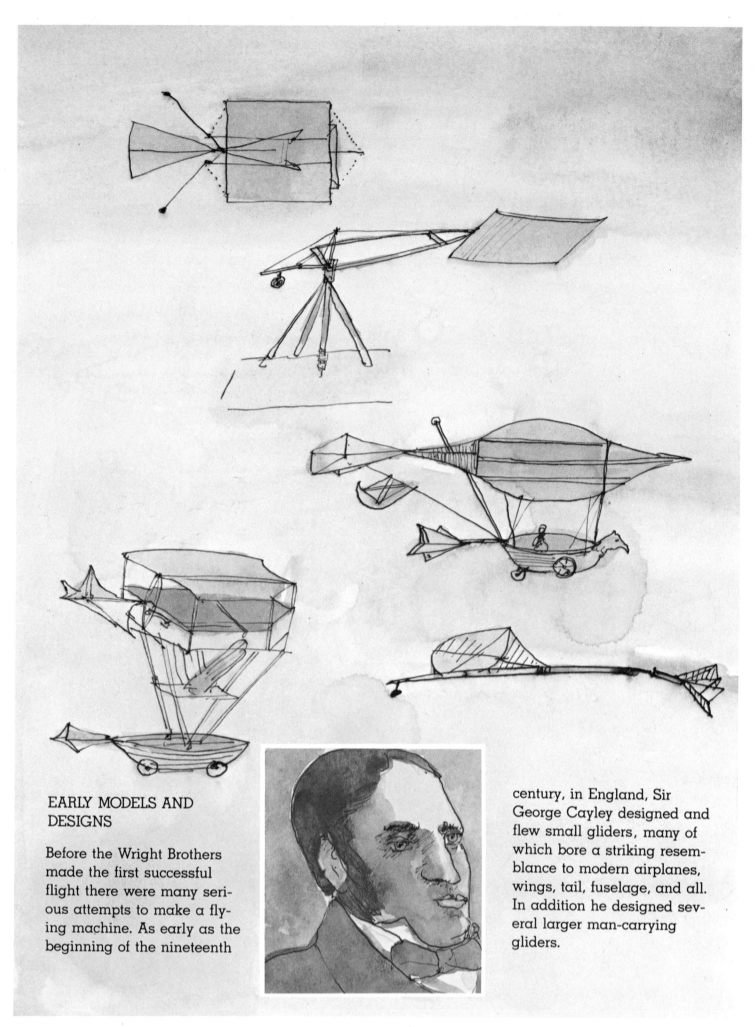

EARLY MODELS AND DESIGNS

Before the Wright Brothers made the first successful flight there were many serious attempts to make a flying machine. As early as the beginning of the nineteenth century, in England, Sir George Cayley designed and flew small gliders, many of which bore a striking resemblance to modern airplanes, wings, tail, fuselage, and all. In addition he designed several larger man-carrying gliders.

CAYLEY'S CONCEPTS FOR FLYING MACHINES.   INSET: SIR GEORGE CAYLEY

By the middle of the nineteenth century, the Englishmen William Samuel Hensen
and John Stringfellow had
drawn (but never flew) several flying-machine designs.
These designs were pub-
lished the world over, inform-
ing the public of what a flying machine might look like.

HENSEN'S CONCEPT FOR FLYING MACHINE

Later the French inventor Alphonse Pénaud built and successfully flew a rubber-band-powered monoplane model with a wing, horizontal tail, fuselage, and pusher propeller.

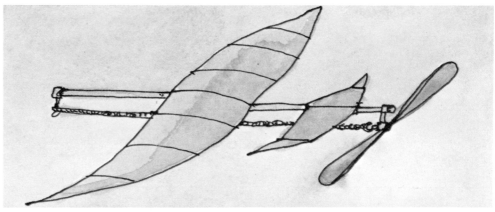

PENAUD MONOPLANE MODEL

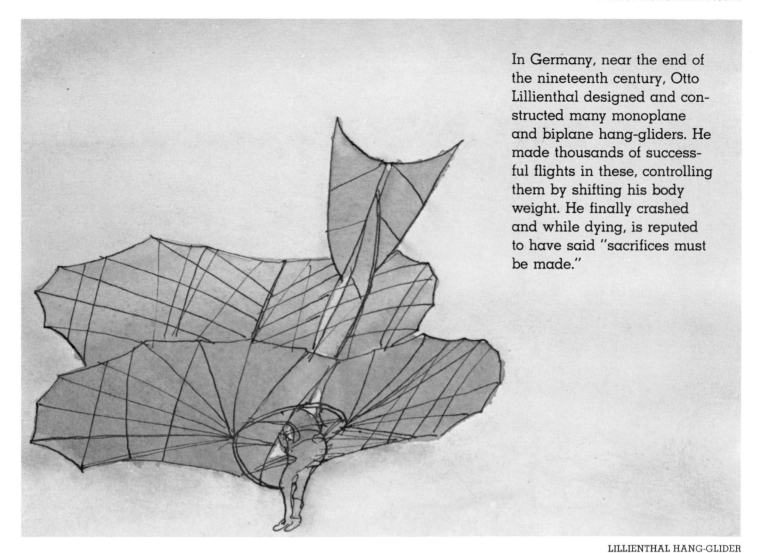

In Germany, near the end of the nineteenth century, Otto Lillienthal designed and constructed many monoplane and biplane hang-gliders. He made thousands of successful flights in these, controlling them by shifting his body weight. He finally crashed and while dying, is reputed to have said "sacrifices must be made."

LILLIENTHAL HANG-GLIDER

During the same period, the Frenchman, Clément Ader built a steam-powered machine which looked like a cross between an airplane and a giant bird. It took off but was incapable of sustained flight.

HOP-FLYER *EOLE* BY CLEMENT ADER

23

In America, as the nineteenth century drew to a close, the Secretary of the Smithsonian Institution, Samuel Pierpont Langley, built and flew some powered flying models. The best of these was about thirteen feet long. It was steam powered and flew for about six-tenths of a mile. Two attempts to perform the same feat in a full-scale manned machine were made. Both ended in failure.

LANGLEY AERODROME ON HOUSEBOAT LAUNCHING PLATFORM

THE WRIGHT BROTHERS

In the United States two bicycle manufacturers from Dayton, Ohio—Wilbur and Orville Wright—had attacked the problems of flight in a totally scientific and technological manner, building and testing models, designing and operating their own wind tunnel, constructing and flying kites, then gliders, and finally airplanes.

WILBUR WRIGHT

ORVILLE WRIGHT

WIND TUNNEL BUILT BY THE WRIGHT BROTHERS

On December 17, 1903 near Kitty Hawk, North Carolina, the Wright Brothers flew successfully in their *Flyer*. In its longest manned flight the 1903 *Flyer* took off, flew under control for 852 feet in fifty-nine seconds, and finally landed on a site not lower than its takeoff site.

WRIGHT BROTHERS' FIRST FLIGHT

In 1905 the Wright Brothers built their *Flyer III* which could fly for half an hour, maneuver in various ways, and perform with unprecedented reliability and consistency. The airplane was here to stay.

WRIGHT *FLYER III*

5. WORLD WAR I

World War I began on August 14, 1914—only eleven years after the Wright brothers' first successful flight—and before long had turned into a brutal ground fight between Germany and the allied forces of France and Great Britain. Both sides dug into elaborate networks of muddy trenches. Small gains of territory were achieved by sending hundreds of thousands of rifle-and bayonet-carrying troops charging directly into enemy machine guns and artillery, always with an appalling loss of life.

FRENCH CAUDRON G.III FLYING OVER TRENCHES

THE AIRPLANE ENTERS THE WAR

For a long while neither side took much notice of what the airplane could do—and as a matter of fact, the primitive planes of 1914 couldn't do very much. But air forces were being formed and soon a growing number of airmen were flying for both sides. At first they flew crude aircraft on observation and artillery-spotting missions. Gradually, the airplanes improved: fighters were manufactured to shoot down the other side's observation planes and to protect their own; and bombers were built to deliver loads of destructive explosives far beyond the range of the largest gun.

The airplane, introduced to combat in World War I, developed during that time into a much more reliable machine, and showed to those with vision what its future wartime role would become.

FRENCH BLERIOT MONOPLANE ON OBSERVATION MISSION

GERMAN TAUBE

EARLY WAR PLANES

One of the most popular aircraft of the early years of World War I was the Etrich Taube, built in Austria and used mainly for observation. *Taube* means dove in German and this airplane was so named because of its unusual wing shape. The trailing wing sections at the tips could be warped by moving a control in the cockpit to provide the kind of lateral or roll control that the Wright brothers had had. On a modern airplane ailerons perform this function.

STABILITY VS. CONTROLLABILITY

As early aviation evolved, a great controversy arose which influenced the design of the warplanes used in World War I. The question was whether a combat airplane should be primarily a stable mode of transportation, like a truck, or an easily maneuverable machine, like a motorcycle.

In the early days of the war, when the airplane was used mainly as an observation outpost, stability was of primary importance.

Both the British B.E.2a and the German Aviatik shown here are examples of such airplanes—stable, lumbering aircraft that later in the war could be shot down easily by any good fighter plane.

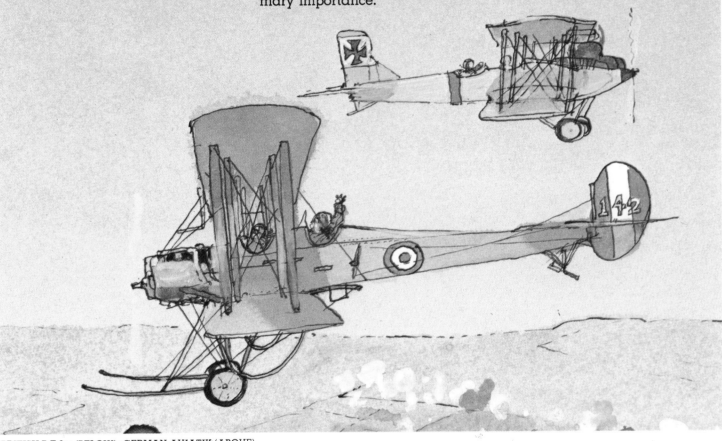

BRITISH B.E.2a (BELOW); GERMAN AVIATIK (ABOVE)

GERMAN FOKKER E.I

As the war progressed, the airplane also became a striking weapon. As a fighter it had to move fast and change course quickly. Maneuverability was essential. The German Fokker E.1 monoplane and its successive versions were responsive, easily maneuvered single-place planes that almost swept the allies from the skies in 1915. This period was known as the "Fokker Scourge."

GERMAN ACES AND PLANES

The pilots with the most victories became known as "aces." The requirements for being an ace varied from country to country, but the aces were always regarded as the best. Germany's greatest early ace, Oswald Boelcke, was modest, brave, and a brilliant strategist. He was a natural leader and was given ever increasing responsibility in the development of the new fighter squadrons. Boelcke is shown here flying an Albatros D.I. fighter. During 1916 Boelcke's fighter was brushed in flight by the plane of one of his own squadron mates. Though appearing to be mild, the collision sent Boelcke's plane out of control and he died in the crash.

OSWALD BOELCKE

BOELCKE'S ALBATROS D.I

The leading pupil of Oswald Boelcke was Max Immelmann, who was credited with developing many of the early fighter tactics including the so-called Immelmann turn. In this maneuver a pursued pilot does a half inside loop and then a half roll placing him above his pursuer and heading in the opposite direction. A plucky pilot might then complete the inside loop, do another half roll, and find himself on the tail of his former pursuer. Here Immelmann is flying an LVG B.I.

IMMELMAN'S LVG B.I (BELOW); BRITISH F.E.2b (ABOVE).   INSET: MAX IMMELMAN

Germany's most celebrated ace was Manfred von Richtofen. Born a "Freiherr" or baron he spent his youth preparing for a military career. After a series of dull assignments early in the war, von Richtofen was made an air observer during which time he applied and was accepted for pilot training. Though a poor flier at first, von Richtofen was an excellent marks-

MANFRED VON RICHTOFEN

man from the start. Before he was shot down on April 21, 1918 he had scored eighty victories, the greatest number of the war. He became known as the Red Baron, the leader of the famous Flying Circus air combat unit. Von Richtofen is shown here flying his all-red Fokker Triplane, the only all-red plane in the air.

RICHTOFEN'S Dr.I FOKKER TRIPLANE

FRENCH ACES AND PLANES

The leading French ace was René Fonck, with seventy-five victories. He bragged about his prowess and was accused of claiming "kills" that he hadn't really made. However, Fonck was undoubtedly a great pilot and marksman.

FONCK'S SPAD XIII.   INSET: RENE FONCK

France's sentimental favorite and second-ranking ace, with fifty-four victories, was Georges Guynemer, the handsome personification of how everyone felt a fighter pilot should look and act.

GUYNEMER'S SPAD.   INSET: GEORGES GUYNEMER

The third-ranking French ace, Charles Nungesser, shown here beside his Nieuport XVII, had forty-five victories to his credit. Note his grisly skull and crossbones, coffin and candles insignia.

NUNGESSER'S NIEUPORT XVII.   INSET: CHARLES NUNGESSER

BRITISH ACES AND PLANES

When World War I began, Edward Mannock, who was to become Britain's leading ace, was interned in Turkey, an ally of Germany. He was returned to England because of his poor health but then obtained a commission in the Royal Engineers and later passed the medical examination for the Royal Flying Corps. He was shot down some months before the war's end after scoring seventy-three victories in the air. Mannock is shown here in a British S.E.5a dogfighting with German Fokker D.VIIs.

MANNOCK IN S.E.5a (ABOVE): GERMAN FOKKERS (BELOW)

EDWARD MANNOCK

Canadian Billy Bishop was Great Britain's second-ranking ace with seventy-two victories. He emerged from the war generally regarded as Britain's authority on air combat.

BILLY BISHOP

BISHOP'S NIEUPORT XVII

James McCudden started his military career as a bugler in 1910. He was a mechanic when the war began and quickly progressed to become a scout pilot. After a highly successful career and fifty-seven victories, McCudden was killed when the engine of his S.E.5a failed during a takeoff.

JAMES McCUDDEN

THE AMERICANS ENTER THE WAR

When the United States entered World War I in April 1917 it had no combat planes to match those in use in Europe, so Americans fought the war in the planes of other countries. Before April 1917 some Americans had already joined air services of the Allied forces. The Lafayette Escadrille was a special squadron in the French air service composed entirely of American pilots.

McCUDDEN IN COCKPIT OF NIEUPORT XVII (BELOW); SIEMENS-SCHUCKERT D.I (ABOVE)

Perhaps the most famous American World War I ace was Eddie Rickenbacker. In 1917 Rickenbacker was a well-known auto racer. He entered the war as a chauffeur on General Pershing's staff but soon became a pilot and was assigned to combat duty. He scored twenty-six victories.

EDDIE RICKENBACKER

RICKENBACKER'S SPAD XIII

Frank Luke, America's second-ranking ace with twenty-one victories, shot down many planes but specialized in attacking enemy observation balloons and sending them down in flames. A loner, he was definitely not an "organization man," and his conformance to military discipline left so much to be desired that he was finally grounded by his commanding officer. Disregarding orders Luke took off, flamed three more German balloons, strafed troops, and when forced to land, fought a number of German soldiers with his service revolver until he was killed. He was posthumously awarded the Congressional Medal of Honor.

GERMAN BALLOON UNDER ATTACK FROM LUKE.   INSET: FRANK LUKE

Raoul Lufbery ran away from home at seventeen to become a world traveler, joined the United States Army, then joined the French Foreign Legion, took flight training and finally was assigned to the Lafayette Escadrille. He scored seventeen victories before he was killed when his Nieuport was set on fire while closing in on a German observation plane.

LUFBERY JUMPING FROM BURNING NIEUPORT.   INSET: RAOUL LUFBERY

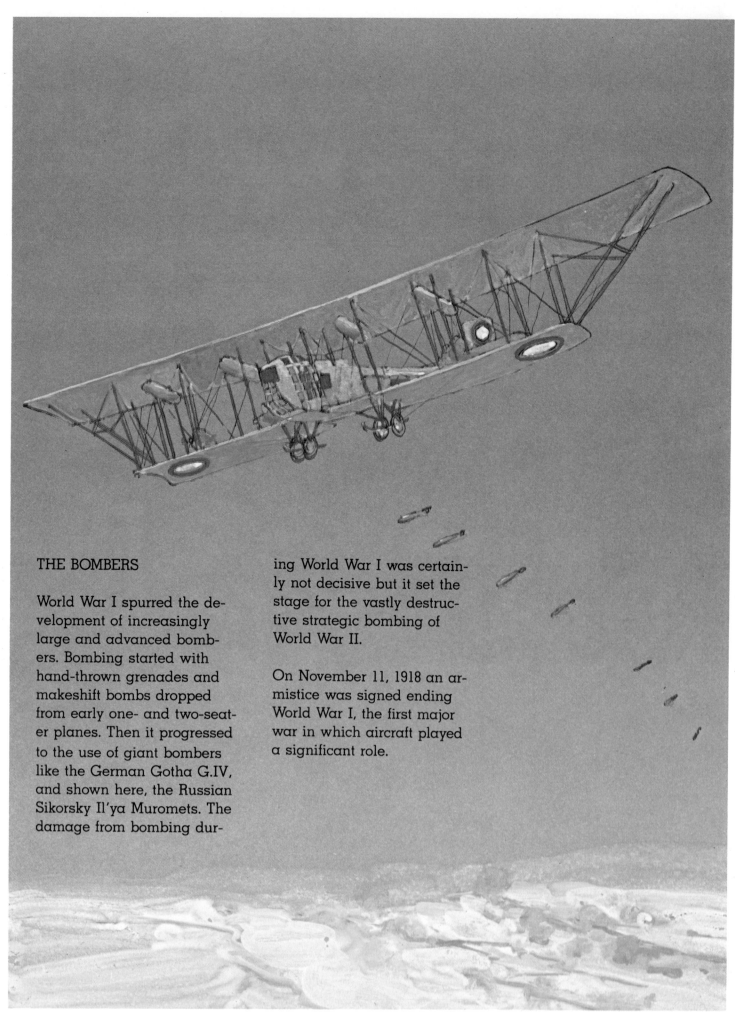

THE BOMBERS

World War I spurred the development of increasingly large and advanced bombers. Bombing started with hand-thrown grenades and makeshift bombs dropped from early one- and two-seater planes. Then it progressed to the use of giant bombers like the German Gotha G.IV, and shown here, the Russian Sikorsky Il'ya Muromets. The damage from bombing during World War I was certainly not decisive but it set the stage for the vastly destructive strategic bombing of World War II.

On November 11, 1918 an armistice was signed ending World War I, the first major war in which aircraft played a significant role.

RUSSIAN IL'YA MUROMETS

6. THE RECORD BREAKERS

Only five or six years after the first Wright Brothers' flight, there were already a substantial number of people able to fly airplanes. Pilots became captivated by the idea of being the first to fly between two places, especially if the flight was to be over water.

COMPETITIONS AND AIR MEETS

In 1909 the London *Daily Mail* offered a £1000 prize to the first aviator to fly across the English Channel. That same year Louis Blériot of France beat his competitors and won the prize despite, some said, the tendency of his Anzani engine to overheat. Here we see Blériot approaching Dover.

LOUIS BLERIOT ON THE FIRST FLIGHT ACROSS THE ENGLISH CHANNEL

REIMS AIR MEET: HUBERT LATHAM IN AN ANTOINETTE IV (ABOVE); GLENN CURTISS IN HIS *GOLDEN FLYER* (BELOW)

Another preoccupation of the early fliers was to see whose machine could fly fastest, farthest, or highest to establish new records. During August of 1909 a week-long air meet was held at Reims, France.

Just about every great aviator in the world was there except the Wright Brothers. New records were set daily and there were many crashes, but, amazingly, no deaths. By the end of the week Glenn Curtiss had flown at forty-three miles an hour and Hubert Latham had flown higher than 500 feet. This illustra-tion shows a spectator's-eye view of some of the airplanes flying past the grandstand. At the top we see Hubert Latham in his Antoinette IV and below him Glenn Curtiss piloting his *Golden Flyer*.

FROM LONDON TO MANCHESTER: PAULHAN IN HIS FARMAN

In 1910 in England the French flyer Louis Paulhan, holder of the world altitude record of 4,165 feet, won £10,000 offered by the *Daily Mail,* for the first flight from London to Manchester.

In October of 1910 a giant international air meet was held at Belmont Park in the United States. The prized Gordon Bennett Trophy went to the popular Englishman Claude Grahame-White for completing the twenty lap course at a dazzling sixty-one miles per hour.

From then on record followed record, sometimes in competition for prizes and sometimes just to enhance the reputation of the pilot or the company that built the plane. World War I brought this kind of flying adventure to an end.

FROM NEWFOUNDLAND TO IRELAND: VICKERS VIMY

TO CROSS THE ATLANTIC

The flying machine emerged from World War I a much more reliable device, capable of longer distance flights and higher speeds. In 1919 the Atlantic Ocean was flown, not once, but three times. First, in May, the U.S. Navy's NC-4 flying-boat flew from Newfoundland to London via the Azores and Lisbon. In June the Englishmen Capt. John Alcock and Lt. Arthur Whitten Brown flew the Atlantic nonstop in a converted Vickers Vimy bomber to win the £10,000 *Daily Mail* prize first offered in 1913. The flight originated in Newfoundland and ended in Ireland sixteen hours later. In July the British dirigible R-34 flew nonstop from Scotland to Mineola, Long Island, and returned nonstop to England.

In 1918 Amelia Earhart served with the Red Cross and while in Canada witnessed a flying exhibition that probably stimulated her desire to become a pilot. She not only became a pilot, she became a great professional pilot.

In 1928 Amelia Earhart flew across the Atlantic as a passenger in a Fokker airplane. Then in 1932, in a red Lockheed Vega, she flew solo from Newfoundland to Ireland in about fifteen hours, becoming the first woman to fly solo across the Atlantic. Later that year she became the first woman to fly solo across the United States.

During the 1919 transatlantic fever, a hotel owner from New York, Raymond Orteig, offered a prize of $25,000 for a nonstop flight between New York and Paris in either direction. Until 1927 no one had been able to perform this feat although there had been some tragic attempts. Then on May 20, 1927, twenty-four-year-old Charles Augustus

Lindbergh, an exbarnstormer, wing walker, and a seasoned airmail pilot, took off in the Ryan NYP *Spirit of St. Louis* from Roosevelt Field, Long Island. The world watched and hoped. In the evening, thirty-three and a half hours later, the *Spirit of St. Louis* landed at Le Bourget Airfield, Paris, and Lindbergh became one of the most adored heroes of modern times.

THE SCHNEIDER AND PULITZER RACES

The races of the mid 1920s and the early 1930s were among the most hotly contested of all racing events and served as a strong stimulant for the development of faster and better airplanes.

Two of the earliest great air competitions were the Schneider and Pulitzer races. The Schneider trophy for seaplanes was established by Frenchman Jacques Schneider. The 1925 Schneider Trophy winner was the American Jimmy Doolittle flying a Curtiss R3C-2 at an average speed of 235 miles per hour.

FROM NEW YORK TO PARIS: *SPIRIT OF ST. LOUIS.*   INSET: CHARLES A. LINDBERGH

In the Schneider races of 1927, 1929, and 1931 England won three times in a row, retiring the trophy. The British Supermarine racers that scored the triple victory were the ancestors of the famous Supermarine Spitfires which performed so well in World War II.

SUPERMARINE S.6

In 1920 the Pulitzer races were established for landplanes by the Pulitzer Brothers of the United States. The brothers, Ralph, Joseph Jr., and Herbert owned and published two American newspapers, the *St. Louis Post-Dispatch* and the New York *World*. The races were an international stimulus to airplane improvements. Here we see the R3C-1, the landplane equivalent of the R3C-2 seaplane that won the Schneider trophy in that same year, 1925. The R3C-1 piloted by Cyrus Bettis won the 1925 Pulitzer Trophy with an average speed of 249 miles per hour.

CURTISS R3C-1

THE BENDIX AND THOMPSON RACES

Two of the best known and highly prized awards were the Bendix and Thompson Trophies. Their golden decade was the 1930s and during this period, speed record after speed record was broken as new and better airplanes and engines were developed.

The Bendix Trophy was awarded to the winner of a transcontinental dash. It was sponsored by the Bendix Aviation Corporation (known for its aircraft instrumentation and led by its President, Mr. Vincent Bendix). Here we see the 1935 Bendix trophy winner *Mr. Mulligan* piloted by Ben Howard.

MR. MULLIGAN

THE GEE BEE

The Thompson Trophy was awarded for the highest speed over a closed course marked by pylons. It was sponsored by Mr. Charles Thompson, president of the famous aircraft equipment manufacturing firm, Thompson Products. Rounding the pylon in this picture is Jimmy Doolittle in the Gee Bee, designed and built by the Granville Brothers. Resembling a barrel with wings, the Gee Bee had a frightful record of fatal crashes and only one known specimen survives today.

CIRCLING THE GLOBE

Once the Atlantic was mastered, fliers were challenged by the thought of circling the globe. In 1924, after 174 days filled with hardship and adventure, four United States Army Air Service pilots in two airplanes completed the first flight around the world. The commanders of the two planes were L.H. Smith and Erik Nelson. The airplanes were the Douglas World Cruisers *Chicago* and *New Orleans*.

DOUGLAS WORLD CRUISERS

The next round-the-world flight, in August 1929, was made from Germany by a dirigible, the *Graf Zeppelin*, which took only a bit over twenty-one days, stopping at Tokyo, Los Angeles, and Lakehurst, New Jersey.

In June of 1931 Wiley Post and Harold Gatty (his navigator), took off from Roosevelt Field, Long Island, in a Lockheed Vega (the famous *Winnie Mae*) for a successful round-the-world flight taking only a little under nine days. In 1933 Wiley Post, this time flying solo, took off from Floyd Bennett Field, Long Island, and flew the *Winnie Mae* around the world in under eight days.

WILEY POST

It was in 1937 while making a round-the-world attempt that Amelia Earhart, America's great woman pilot, was lost in the Pacific with Fred Noonan her navigator while trying to find tiny Howland Island.

By 1938 the American Howard Hughes and a crew of four were able to circumnavigate the globe in a twin-engine Lockheed in less than four days.

Today, with routine in-flight refueling for airplanes, and with satellites that can circle the earth in minutes, flying around the world has lost much of its original significance.

AMELIA EARHART

7. EARLY AIR TRANSPORTATION

FLYING THE MAIL

As soon as airplanes could carry cargo, mail was considered a prime choice for the new service.

The first shipment of mail, from Washington D.C. to New York, was sent off in a Curtiss JN-4H on May 15, 1918 with appropriate ceremony, but the pilot got lost by following the wrong railroad track, and the mail had to be returned to Washington by truck. The second shipment also got lost. Then things began to straighten out.

It was the early airmail pilots who pioneered the first air routes, navigating initially by sighting railroad tracks, highways, and bonfires, and later, beacons, then gradually being guided by an increasingly more sophisticated air traffic control system. Here we see a Douglas M-2 mailplane flying over a bonfire marker.

DOUGLAS M-2 MAILPLANE

THE TRIMOTORS

During the 1920s and early 1930s a family of planes made by various manufacturers evolved. They had three engines—one mounted on the nose of the fuselage and one mounted on each wing. The most famous of these trimotors were those made by Fokker, and by Ford in the United States. The Fokker trimotor could carry about ten passengers, cruised at about 100 miles per hour, and was of more or less conventional construction. The Ford trimotor was called the Tin Goose and it is best recognized by its corrugated metal skin. The Tin Goose was a no frills airplane with wicker seats and minimum passenger comforts, but good safety. In all, nearly 100 companies used Ford trimotors in passenger service.

FORD TRIMOTOR

THE FABULOUS H.P. 42/45

The Handley Page H.P.42/45 Class biplane was the first four-engine design ever made expressly for passenger service. In England in the early 1930s, Handley Page built eight in two versions, the Eastern H.P.42 and the Western H.P.45. The Eastern models did well on the long London-Cairo-Capetown-Karachi route while the Western models were suited to the short London-Paris route.

These huge luxurious airplanes featured hot meals and a bar in flight, and while very slow (they cruised at about 100 miles per hour), they were economical to operate. Above all they were safe and established a record of no passenger fatalities throughout the period of their use.

HANDLEY PAGE WESTERN MODEL H.P. 45

IMPERIAL AIRWAYS

G-AAGX

HANDLEY PAGE EASTERN MODEL H.P. 42

THE DC-3

In 1933 the Douglas Aircraft Company built a prototype of a nearly all metal, very streamlined transport airplane, the twin-engined DC-1, intended to be far superior to any airplane then in use. This design, with some improvements, became the DC-2 and about 200 of these were built. In response to a specific request from American Airlines, the wider bodied sleeper-plane, the DST, was created in 1935, and from this was developed the immortal DC-3, the plane that changed air transportation forever.

Its design was so superior that by the late 1930s the DC-3 was the standard transport on nearly every scheduled airline. It had a rugged structure that could withstand abuse and metal fatigue damage like no other, it was most forgiving of pilot error, and handled easily under all normal conditions. It weighed about 26,000 pounds and could carry a payload of 9,000 pounds cargo or (generally) twenty-one passengers. About 14,000 DC-3s (or their Russian copies, the Li-2) were built and many are still in service.

DOUGLAS DC-3 SKIRTING A STORM

LOCKHEED CONSTELLATION TAKING OFF

THE CONSTELLATION

The Lockheed Constellation first flew in 1943 and it looked different from the start. It had three vertical tails and a graceful S-curved fuselage. There were those who thought it the most graceful transport that had ever flown. In some of its advanced versions it could carry about 100 passengers. With a maximum range of about 6000 miles it could even outdistance its closest competitor the Douglas DC-7C.

Even after jets came in, Constellations hung on for years, but now seeing a Connie in flight is a real rarity.

8. WORLD WAR II

INVASION BY GERMANY

In the 1920s and 1930s, although forbidden by the Treaty of Versailles, Germany had been secretly developing an air force which by the late 1930s had become the most powerful in the world. In September of 1939 Germany attacked Poland. Great Britain and France responded by declaring war on Germany. World War II had begun.

GERMAN JUNKERS Ju 87

By the second day of the war, the mighty German air force, the Luftwaffe, had gained total control of the skies over Poland. From then on, it took the Germans less than a week to decimate Polish defenses. The complete conquest of Poland took about one month. This was the German "blitzkrieg" or lightning war, a coordinated attack of air forces, ground troops, and armed vehicles. To the left we see German Junkers Ju 87 "Stuka" dive bombers attacking a target as the tanks prepare to move in.

In rapid succession the apparently undefeatable German war machine conquered Norway, Denmark, Holland, Luxembourg, Belgium, and France. In all of these major actions, German air power provided control of the skies so that the tanks, motorized forces, paratroops, and armies could perform their deadly functions below. How different from World War I in which airplanes were initially regarded only as mobile observation posts.

In the early part of World War II bombers like the Heinkel He 111, Junkers Ju 88, and Dornier Do 17, vigorously attacked ground targets while they were guarded by swarms of powerful fighters like the Messerschmitt Bf 109 and Bf 110.

HEINKEL He 111

JUNKERS Ju 88

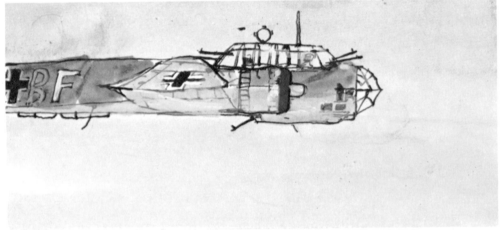

DORNIER Do 17

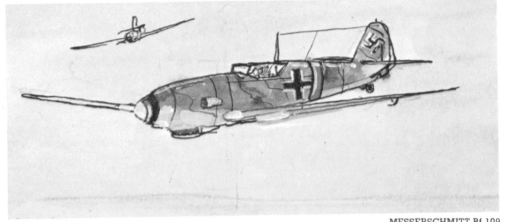

MESSERSCHMITT Bf 109

THE BATTLE OF BRITAIN

With the fall of France in the summer of 1940, the Battle of Britain began. Germany and her new ally, Italy, expected to invade England as soon as the Royal Air Force was wiped out. A maximum effort was begun to decimate the RAF and all of its airfields and installations. Then, slowly, came the big surprise. After years of unpreparedness, Britain had finally developed a defense system. A network of radar stations, ground observers, filter centers, and command centers was set up to detect and follow incoming German air raids.

Here we see the interior of a British command center with its plotting tables and wall plots showing the locations and directions of approaching attacking planes. The staffs of these centers were able to send RAF Spitfire and Hurricane fighters out with specific directions for finding and engaging the enemy planes. The British had also succeeded in breaking the German code, considerably helping efforts to learn where the bombers intended to strike.

After suffering increasing losses the Luftwaffe changed its tactics and began to bomb the cities of England, a strategy that would kill thousands of civilians but would also stiffen the British resistance. In October 1940 Hitler postponed his invasion plans indefinitely and the RAF had won the Battle of Britain—a most unusual battle in which massive air fleets fought each other daily and in which infantry, battleships, and tanks had practically nothing to do with the final outcome.

BRITISH COMMAND CENTER

JAPANESE AICHI D3A1 TAKING OFF FROM CARRIER FOR PEARL HARBOR ATTACK

PEARL HARBOR

On December 7, 1941 Japan entered World War II with a surprise air attack on the United States military and naval installations at and around Pearl Harbor in the Hawaiian Islands. The attacking planes, launched from six Japanese aircraft carriers, included fighters like the famous Mitsubishi A6M2, dive bombers such as the Aichi D3A1, and torpedo bombers such as the Nakajima B5N2. Our code names for these three planes were Zero (or Zeke), Val, and Kate. The Pearl Harbor attack took the American forces totally by surprise, putting all of the American battleships out of action and sinking cruisers and lesser ships. Fortunately, the aircraft carriers *Enterprise* and *Lexington* were at sea and survived the massacre.

The rampaging Japanese air forces then sank, in short order, most of the British sea power in the Pacific including the battleships *Prince of Wales* and *Repulse*, the carrier *Hermes*, and many lesser but important ships.

DOUGLAS TBD TORPEDO BOMBER

CORAL SEA AND MIDWAY

The Japanese war machine raged on in the Pacific Ocean area, conquering the Philippine Islands, Hong Kong, Singapore, Malaya, Burma, and Borneo, and continuing its movement in the direction of Australia by sending an invasion fleet against Port Moresby in New Guinea. This led to the Battle of the Coral Sea in May 1942 in which the Japanese fleet won a tactical victory by sinking the American carrier *Lexington*, the destroyer *Sims*, and the tanker *Neosho*, while the Japanese suffered only the loss of the light carrier *Shoho* and damage to the fleet carrier *Shokaku*. This battle was the first in which no ship on either side saw an enemy ship. The action was plane vs. plane and plane vs. ship. The American planes in this battle were the Douglas SBD Dauntless dive bomber, a truly great plane, the Douglas TBD Devastator torpedo bomber, and the Grumman F4F Wildcat, a fighter weaker than the Japanese A6M2 Zero, but the best the American forces had at the time. But, uncertain of the strength of the Allied forces, the Japanese invasion fleet turned back. It was this withdrawal which provided the first glimmer of hope for the Allied cause.

Then the Japanese made their fatal mistake. They launched an attack against Midway Island, a key stronghold in the mid-Pacific. This led to a naval battle and defeat which cost the Japanese most of their fleet-sized carrier strength. It was the turning point in the sea warfare in the Pacific.

NORTH AFRICA, SICILY, AND ITALY

In the intense heat of the North African desert the tankers had their war with the advantage shifting between the Allied and Axis powers, sometimes overnight. Always, air power was vital.

North Africa became a springboard first to the conquest of Sicily and then to all of Italy.

CURTISS P-40s

BOEING B-17

CONSOLIDATED B-24

NORTH AMERICAN B-25

ALLIED INVASION

As World War II progressed, the Allies developed and ran an arsenal which manufactured planes, tanks, and guns at a rate never dreamed of before. The production of machines such as America's Boeing B-17 Flying Fortresses, Consolidated B-24 Liberators, Boeing B-29 Superfortresses, North American B-25 Mitchells, Douglas A-26 Invaders, Republic P-47 Thunderbolts,

REPUBLIC P-47

North American P-51 Mustangs, British Avro Lancasters, Handley Page Halifaxes, Vickers Wellingtons, de Havilland Mosquitos, Supermarine Spitfires, Hawker Typhoons, and the like was overwhelming. This sealed the doom of the Axis powers.

On June 6, 1944, D day, the Allied invasion of Europe began under a canopy of Allied air power.

NORTH AMERICAN P-51

AVRO LANCASTER

SUPERMARINE SPITFIRE

HAWKER TYPHOON

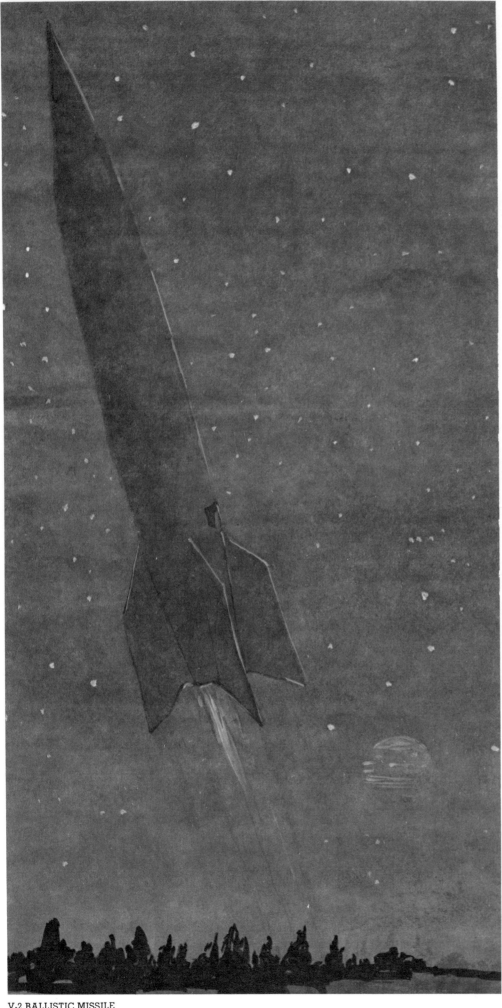

V-2 BALLISTIC MISSILE

The invasion progressed across Europe. Germany, in desperation, introduced some revolutionary technical developments like the Messerschmitt Me 163 rocket-powered interceptor, the Messerschmitt Me 262 jet-powered fighter and the Junkers Ju 287 heavy jet bomber. Germany also introduced her "Vengeance Weapons," the V-1 buzz bomb and the V-2 ballistic missile. All of this was to no avail and on May 7, 1945, Germany surrendered.

GIANT AIR RAIDS

A great tragedy of World War I was the sending of thousands, actually hundreds of thousands, of troops out of the trenches into almost certain death by enemy machine gun and artillery fire. A great tragedy of World War II was the use of massive air raids (some involving over a thousand planes) directed at the hearts of the world's major cities. These raids were devastating, but subsequent analyses have shown that civilian morale, even under these perilous circumstances, generally remained high.

Toward the end of the Battle of Britain the Germans began to bomb London heavily. Raids were then mounted against most British cities, including, on the night of November 14, 1940 a particularly vicious, destructive raid against the cathedral town of Coventry.

As the war progressed, the Allies sent raids of thousands of planes against German cities like Cologne, Dusseldorf, and Dresden. These raids, with their deployment of thousands of tons of explosives and incendiary devices, turned cities into infernos and created a new meteorological phenomenon, the firestorm.

COVENTRY CATHEDRAL AFTER AIR RAID

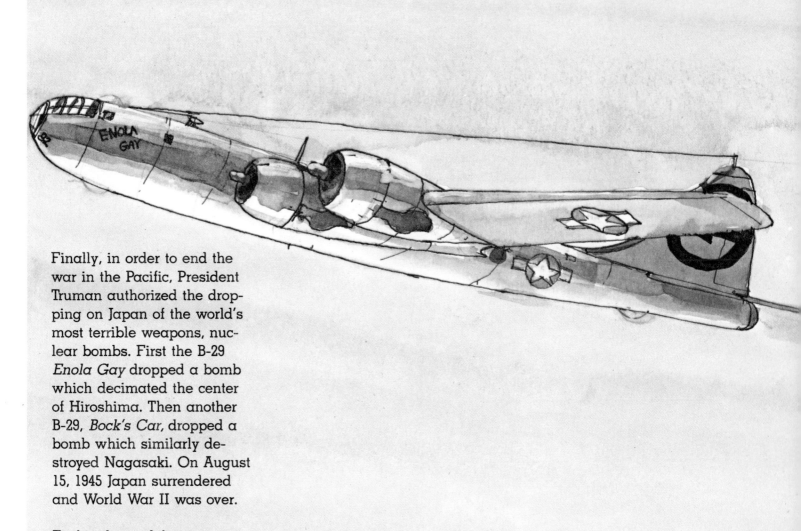

Finally, in order to end the war in the Pacific, President Truman authorized the dropping on Japan of the world's most terrible weapons, nuclear bombs. First the B-29 *Enola Gay* dropped a bomb which decimated the center of Hiroshima. Then another B-29, *Bock's Car,* dropped a bomb which similarly destroyed Nagasaki. On August 15, 1945 Japan surrendered and World War II was over.

To this day a debate rages over whether the avoidance of an invasion of Japan and the saving of perhaps millions of Allied lives was worth the terrible death dropped on these two Japanese cities.

BOEING B-29: *ENOLA GAY*

THE ACES

Few of the pilots of World War II attained the fame of the aces of World War I; however they fought just as valiantly. Pictured here are some of the leading aces of the various countries.

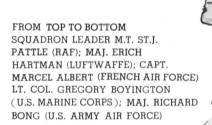

FROM TOP TO BOTTOM
SQUADRON LEADER M.T. ST.J.
PATTLE (RAF); MAJ. ERICH
HARTMAN (LUFTWAFFE); CAPT.
MARCEL ALBERT (FRENCH AIR FORCE)
LT. COL. GREGORY BOYINGTON
(U.S. MARINE CORPS); MAJ. RICHARD
BONG (U.S. ARMY AIR FORCE)

9. FLIGHT OPERATIONS AT SEA

USS *KITTY HAWK*

What floats on water, weighs about seventy thousand tons, looks like a postage stamp as you approach it from the air, feeds and sleeps about five thousand people for months at a time, can safely halt a moving fifty-thousand-pound airplane in a few hundred feet, and serves as a home base for about ninety aircraft? That's right, an aircraft carrier, the most important kind of ship in World War II and still an indispensible component of air and sea power.

CURTISS BIPLANE TAKING OFF FROM USS *BIRMINGHAM*

CURTISS BIPLANE LANDING ON USS *PENNSYLVANIA*

AIRCRAFT CARRIER BEGINNINGS

The first successful "aircraft carrier takeoff" occurred in November of 1910 after the cruiser U.S.S. *Birmingham* had been modified by having an eighty-three-foot, flat wooden platform erected over her foredeck. While the *Birmingham* was cruising near Hampton Roads, Virginia, Eugene Ely climbed into a Curtiss biplane, applied full power, rolled along the wood- en platform, dropped peril- ously close to the water, then flew to land.

Two months later the very same Eugene Ely took off from San Francisco, Califor- nia, flew thirteen miles out to sea, then landed on a make- shift wooden deck which had been erected over the stern of The U.S.S. *Pennsylvania*. On each side of the deck were sandbags connected in pairs by ropes stretched across it. As Ely touched the deck, hooks on his landing gear engaged the ropes and sand- bags, accumulating and dragging them until he stopped. This was the first aircraft landing on a ship. The equipment used was very crude by modern stan- dards, but the system was one similar in basic concept to the arresting gear used on carriers today.

THE FIRST AMERICAN AIRCRAFT CARRIER

During World War I the British had developed two aircraft carriers, the H.M.S. *Argus* and the H.M.S. *Furious*. Then in 1919, the Director of U.S. Naval Aviation requested that the *Jupiter* (a coal carrier which had been commissioned in 1913 and had served during the First World War) be converted to become America's first aircraft carrier. Her name was changed to the U.S.S. *Langley*, in honor of the distinguished pre-Wright brothers experimenter Samuel Pierpont Langley, and she was used as a floating laboratory to develop American naval aviation. Below decks her thirty to fifty planes were moved around by traveling cranes and raised to the flight deck by an elevator.

In 1927 new carriers joined the American fleet, much improved by all the lessons learned on the *Langley*. By World War II even more efficient carriers had been developed and the old lady *Langley* was converted to a seaplane tender. In 1942 while she was carrying fighter planes to Java, Japanese bombers caught up with the *Langley* and turned her into a smoking wreck. She died fighting.

USS *JUPITER*

USS *LANGLEY*

EARLY UNITED STATES NAVY CARRIER AIRCRAFT

The first aircraft to operate off carriers were conventional biplanes with hooks added to catch the carrier's primitive arresting gear. By the end of the 1920s specially designed airplanes like the Boeing F4B-4 fighter made the carrier pilot, according to some, "a member of the best flying club in the world."

BOEING F4B-4

The Martin T3M-1, in service during the late twenties, was one of the early torpedo bombers. Its main mission was to skim just over the waves with a torpedo slung under its fuselage to launch against an enemy ship. Torpedo bombing proved to be a very dangerous mission. The T3M-1 shown here is taking off from the deck of the carrier *Lexington*.

MARTIN T3M-1 TAKING OFF FROM USS *LEXINGTON*

The last important pre-World War II Navy biplane fighter was the Grumman F3F-1, shown here with tail hook extended, just before touching down on the old U.S.S. *Enterprise.* After the hook engaged one of the arresting-gear cables stretched across the after section of the flight deck, the momentum of the airplane pulled the cable out, driving an arresting engine which stopped the plane in a short distance.

GRUMMAN F3F-1 ON FINAL APPROACH

GRUMMAN F4F (ABOVE); MITSUBISHI ZERO (BELOW)

WORLD WAR II CARRIERS AND THEIR AIRCRAFT

The Japanese Navy launched its disastrous attack against Pearl Harbor on December 7, 1941. This surprise attack came entirely from carrier-based aircraft launched from Japan's six major carriers: the *Kaga, Akagi, Soryu, Hiryu, Shokaku,* and *Zuikaku.* During World War II the aircraft carrier would become the backbone of sea power in the Pacific for both the American and Japanese navies.

An early hint of the carriers' importance was the April 1942 raid on various cities in Japan, including Tokyo, by sixteen North American B-25 Mitchell bombers led by the famous Jimmy Doolittle. The big planes barely got off the carrier *Hornet,* bombed carefully selected targets in Japan, and were deliberately crash-landed or abandoned in flight when their fuel gave out over China. Most of the American pilots were saved, and the raid gave Japan a stunning psychological shock.

FAIREY SWORDFISH TORPEDO BOMBER

NORTH AMERICAN B-25s TAKING OFF FROM USS *HORNET*

MIDWAY: THE CARRIERS SLUG IT OUT

During the early portion of World War II the Japanese fleet commander, Admiral Yamamoto, believed that his fleet must strike at the American base on Midway Island, and by so doing, provoke a decisive action with the units of the U.S. Navy which still remained afloat after the disaster at Pearl Harbor. Yamamoto believed that at Midway he could completely annihilate the American fleet.

But the Americans had acquired an advantage—they had broken the Japanese code. They knew that an attack against Midway was coming although they could not be sure of many of the important details, such as the exact location of the attacking Japanese fleet.

In early June, 1942 two task forces containing the three American carriers, *Yorktown, Enterprise,* and *Hornet,* waited and searched near Midway Island for the Japanese fleet. When the fleet was sighted, American land-based planes were sent out from Midway Island to attack. Then the planes from the American carriers were launched. Forty-one torpedo bombers accompanied by all the available Wildcat fighters arrived first to attack the Japanese fleet. But despite the protection of the Wildcat fighters, the torpedo bombers were slaughtered and no damage was inflicted on the Japanese ships.

At this dramatic moment, when all seemed lost, in came the carrier-based American dive bombers. The fifty-four Douglas Dauntless SBDs sent out by the carriers *Enterprise* and *Yorktown* inflicted mortal damage on the *Kaga, Akagi,* and *Soryu,* half of Japan's operational fleet

carriers. This action is shown here. Subsequently, dive bombers struck the carrier *Hiryu* which sank some hours later. The American force lost only the carrier *Yorktown.*

After this absolute disaster, Japanese dominance of the Pacific Ocean ended, and the Japanese forces would never approach superiority again.

DOUGLAS SBD DIVE BOMBERS ATTACKING JAPANESE CARRIERS

GRUMMAN F6F SHOOTING DOWN A JAPANESE ZERO-SEN A6M5

THE MARIANAS TURKEY SHOOT

Near the end of World War II there was another battle in the Pacific that ended in an overwhelming victory for Allied carrier airpower. The action began in June, 1944 with amphibious landings on the islands Saipan, Guam, and Tinian in the Marianas. The outnumbered Japanese threw everything they had into the battle including five battleships and nine aircraft carriers plus hundreds of land-based planes. The Grumman F6F Hellcats, Chance Vought F4U Corsairs, and other American carrier planes had a field day against the best that Japan could send into this monster of a sea and air battle. The Japanese lost 366 planes, the Americans twenty-six. No wonder it was called the Marianas Turkey Shoot by the American forces. Shown here is an F6F Hellcat shooting down a Japanese Mitsubishi A6M5.

MODERN CARRIER OPERATIONS

A Grumman F-14 Tomcat fighter is shown here after being launched from the giant carrier, *America.* Other aircraft wait their turn for launching on the forward deck. An angled deck aft of the forward deck is used primarily for landing (the Navy calls it recovery). If the tail hook of a landing plane has missed all of the arresting cables strung across the angled deck, the plane is in perfect position for an unobstructed emergency takeoff under its own full power, an important safety feature of modern aircraft carrier operations.

GRUMMAN F-14 LAUNCHED FROM CARRIER

10. HELICOPTERS

The most common way to make a flyable aircraft is to provide it with wings and a propulsive system like an engine and propeller. Then when the propeller forces the airplane to move through the air, the wings will produce lift and support the flying airplane against the downward pull of the earth's gravity.

However, suppose we want to make a flying machine that will hover, that is, a machine that will remain up in the air even though it is not moving through it. The fixed wings of an airplane simply won't produce lift unless the airplane is moving through the air at a reasonable speed. An airplane stopped in flight would simply dive or glide directly to earth.

One way to make a flying machine hover is to move its wings without moving the rest of the machine. How do we do that? We give our machine rotating wings and we call the machine a helicopter.

A MECHANICAL AND A NATURAL HOVERER

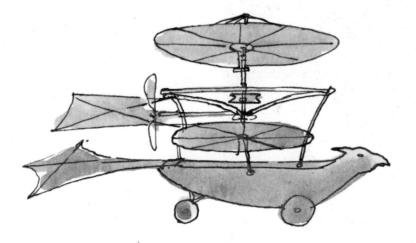

The helicopter idea is not new. The great thinker Leonardo da Vinci sketched a kind of helicopter in the late fifteenth century. Sir George Cayley, improving upon an eighteenth century French model by Launoy and Bienvenu, flew a helicopter model in the early nineteenth century. In 1907 the Frenchman Paul Cornu built a two-rotor helicopter which briefly lifted a man off the ground.

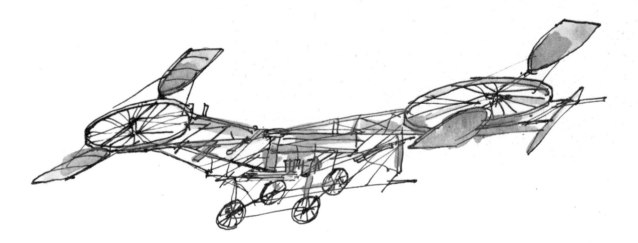

Then why did we have to wait until 1939 for Igor Sikorsky to develop the first practical helicopter? The answer is stability and control. If we merely rotate two or three wings, each attached at one end to a shaft, we can create lift, but we find that the device may rise unsteadily off the ground, perhaps tip over and fall back to earth. What was needed was a controllable and stable rotating wing design that would allow the craft to either hover, move directionally, or climb and descend at will without the introduction of any unwanted motions.

HELICOPTER CONCEPTS: CAYLEY (TOP); CORNU (CENTER); LEONARDO DA VINCI (BOTTOM)

FOCKE-ACHGELIS Fw-61

In 1938 in Berlin the Focke-Achgelis Fw-61 helicopter shown here flew for the public inside the Deutschland-halle indoor arena. Piloted by a woman, Hanna Reitsch, the machine took off, hovered, maneuvered, and landed. The Focke-Achgelis machine did not carry a substantial payload and was therefore not quite a practical machine.

SIKORSKY VS-300

In 1939 Igor Sikorsky flew a helicopter of his own design which had superior controllability and the potential for carrying a payload. This machine was the Sikorsky VS-300, the world's first "practical" helicopter, and it started a whole new industry.

The diversity of helicopter designs is impressive. Some have a single rotor overhead to whirl the rotating wings or blades. This variety (like the Sikorsky R-4 shown here) needs a small tail rotor to keep the machine from turning in a direction opposite to that of the main rotor. The Sikorsky R-4 was the first successful operational helicopter.

SIKORSKY R-4

The tandem rotor helicopter has two equal-sized rotors, one at the front and one at the rear. The Piasecki HRP-1 was the first practical tandem-rotor helicopter. Since the front and rear rotors are designed to whirl in opposite directions, it doesn't need an extra rotor to keep the body from turning.

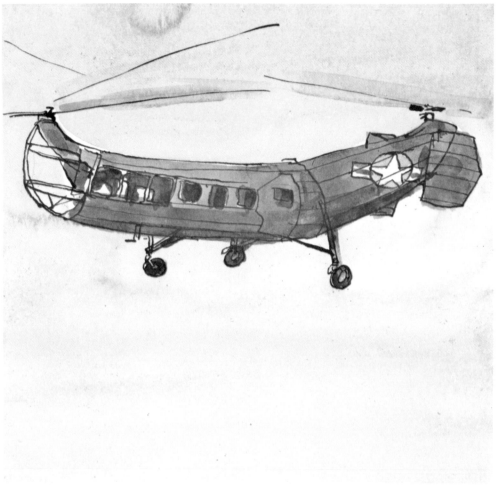

PIASECKI HRP-1

Yet another helicopter design employs two identical rotors which revolve in opposite directions on the same or nearby shafts with their blades meshed to prevent them from interfering with each other. The Kaman line of helicopters included a few designs of this type such as the Huskie rescue helicopter shown here, but the type has lost popularity in recent years.

KAMAN HUSKIE

A special variety of the main-and-tail-rotor type of helicopter has been widely used for many years. This design features a two-bladed main rotor, steadied by an auxiliary dynamic balance system. The various Bell Helicopter models from the long-lived and popular Model 47 to the civil Model 214 and the military model Huey Cobra, exemplify the two-bladed rotor type of design.

BELL HUEY COBRA

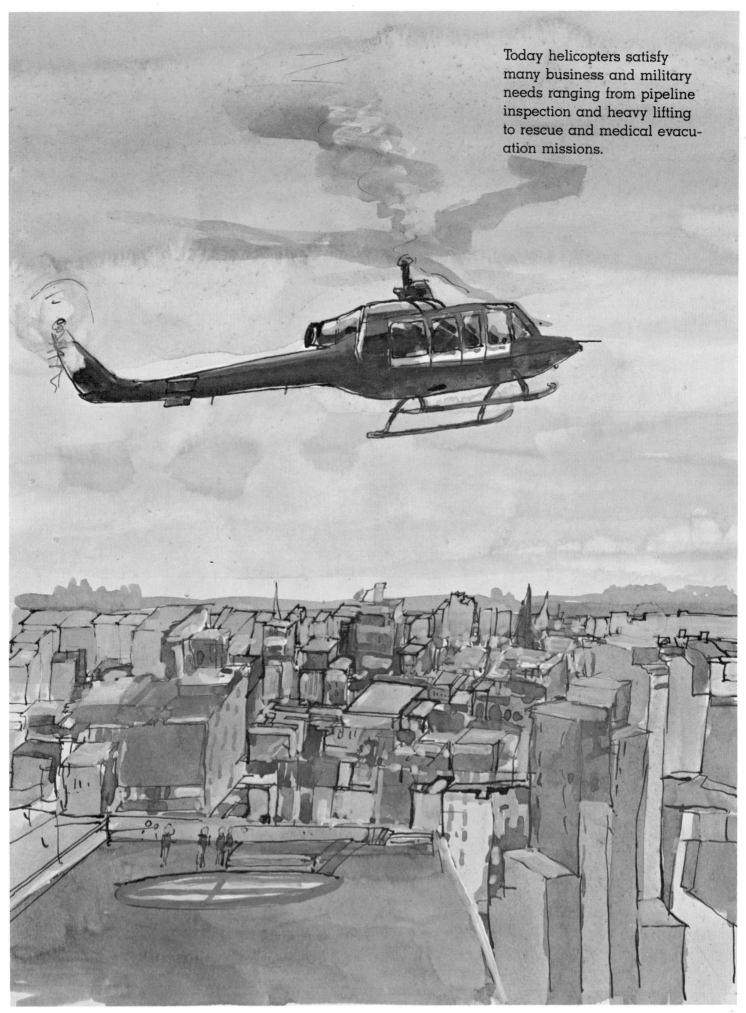

Today helicopters satisfy many business and military needs ranging from pipeline inspection and heavy lifting to rescue and medical evacuation missions.

BELL MODEL 214

11. OFF THE BEATEN TRACK

Some airplanes look very different from others and engineers sometimes say that if an airplane looks like it won't fly well, it generally won't.

It's difficult to measure the contributions made by these unconventional airplane designs. Some led nowhere while others achieved some success or even had great influence over future designs.

Consider the first airplane to take off from water. It was engineered and first flown on March 28, 1910 by Henri Fabre of France. The tail surfaces were mounted on the front of the plane, while the wing, engine, and propeller were at the rear. This strange looking but successful airplane was supported by three floats attached under the main structure and must be regarded as the ancestor of all floatplanes.

FABRE FLOATPLANE TAKING OFF

PLANES FOR AIRBORNE AIRCRAFT CARRIERS

During the late 1920s and early 1930s some designers began thinking of using dirigibles as aircraft carriers. After all, they could go anywhere in the "ocean of air" and cruise at about sixty miles per hour.

What kind of plane should be built to operate from a dirigible? It would need wheels for airport takeoffs and landings, and it would also need a mechanism by which it could hook onto a "trapeze" as it flew under the dirigible to be pulled up inside.

The Curtiss F9C Sparrow-hawk was designed for the job and it was a fine little plane. But dirigibles proved to be impractical. They were hard to handle on the ground in even moderately gusty weather, they could break up in flight from turbulence caused by storms, and if they used hydrogen as their lifting gas they could explode. Dirigibles didn't become airborne aircraft carriers after all, and so the F9C was an unneeded airplane.

CURTISS F9C HOOKING-UP UNDER A DIRIGIBLE

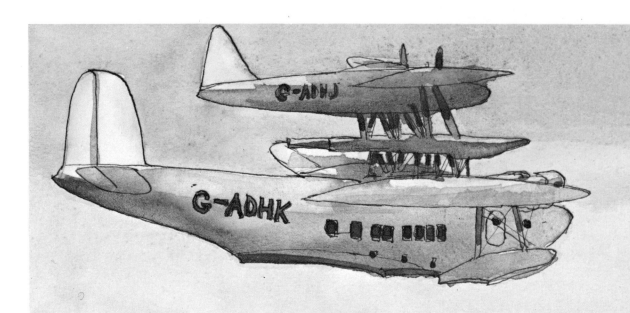

PIGGYBACK

In the mid-1930s the problem of how to make an airplane that could fly the Atlantic Ocean nonstop with a profitable payload was a challenge for manufacturers of commercial planes. Short Brothers and Harland of Northern Ireland came up with a really imaginative but impractical solution—the *Mayo* composite.

The scheme required two airplanes, a big flying-boat, the *Maia*, and a smaller floatplane, the *Mercury* which rode piggyback on the top of the *Maia* during takeoff. The fully loaded *Mercury* would be carried up near cruise altitude by the *Maia* which would then release it and land while the *Mercury* continued across the Atlantic. The theory behind this combination was that the *Maia* would consume the fuel needed for takeoff and climb,

allowing the *Mercury*, once it was released, to use all of its fuel for the flight over the ocean. On July 21, 1938 a successful crossing was made.

But big, long-range airplanes proved to be the simpler, more efficient solution, so the *Mayo* composite idea was abandoned after its one successful trial.

MAYO COMPOSITE

A FLYING AUTO

The Waterman Arrowbile was basically an automobile to which a wing-tail assembly could be attached, turning it into an airplane. Its Studebaker engine could drive its wheels or its propeller. The idea was to fly it from airport to airport, then remove the wings and tail converting the body to an automobile for trips into nearby towns. The Waterman Arrowbile flew well and got great publicity, but the idea never caught on.

WATERMAN ARROWBILE

STRANGE FIGHTERS

The Northrop XP-56 was a tailless experimental fighter. An odd design with bent wings, underslung fin, and pusher propeller, it never flew well and the design was dropped.

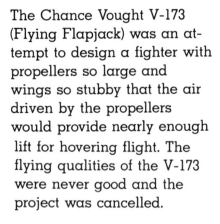

NORTHROP XP-56

The Chance Vought V-173 (Flying Flapjack) was an attempt to design a fighter with propellers so large and wings so stubby that the air driven by the propellers would provide nearly enough lift for hovering flight. The flying qualities of the V-173 were never good and the project was cancelled.

CHANCE VOUGHT V-173

The Convair XFY-1 (Pogo) was to be a shipboard fighter that didn't need a flight deck. It was to take off and land on a small topside platform, resting on its tail when not in flight. It was flight tested but was never good enough to be put into production.

CONVAIR XFY-1

87

DORNIER DoX

THE X AIRPLANES

During the 1940s a number of aeronautical engineers tried to design a plane that would go faster in level flight than the speed of sound. The speed of sound is about 760 miles per hour at sea level and decreases somewhat as a plane flies at higher and higher altitudes. Up until the 1940s, flying at such speed was regarded as somewhere between difficult, dangerous, and impossible. There was even talk of a "sound barrier" that might keep an airplane from flying faster than the speed of sound. However, this proved to be unfounded and the first plane to succeed, on October 14, 1947, was a rocket-propelled airplane shaped something like a bullet with wings. This plane was first designated the Bell XS-1 but was later changed to X-1. The pilot was Chuck Yeager, then a Captain in the Air Force. This great X-1 achievement ushered in the era of supersonic flight.

MONSTERS

The German Dornier DoX was developed in the late 1920s. This giant flying-boat, built to carry about 150 passengers, had twelve engines and was still underpowered. The DoX did make a round-trip flight from Germany to the United States but with many problems. Had the engines been more powerful the DoX might have succeeded and revolutionized air transportation.

The Hughes-Kaiser HK-1 (Hercules) was conceived during World War II by the eccentric millionaire Howard

Hughes working with Henry J. Kaiser, the dynamic World War II shipbuilder. This eight-engined giant was built to carry about 700 troops or many tons of supplies over submarine-infested waters. The HK-1 (sometimes known as the H-4) was the largest airplane ever built. It was made primarily of noncritical materials, principally wood, earning it the nickname "spruce goose," a term that offended Howard Hughes, especially since the wood in the HK-1 was mostly birch not spruce!

The X-1 was followed by a series of X airplanes, including the X-2, an even faster rocket plane, the X-3, a needle-nosed jet with stubby ultrathin wings, the X-4, a tailless jet, the X-5, the first swing-wing airplane, and a number of other advanced planes and rockets. The experimental "X" programs also provided a wealth of wind-tunnel and flight-test data which has proved useful in the analysis of many new aircraft designs, as well as in the development of improved analytic methods.

HUGHES HK-1

BELL X-I

BELL X-2 (ABOVE); BELL X-5 (BELOW)

12. MILITARY JETS

The jet engine was invented independently in England and in Germany just prior to World War II. It offered the possibility of great speed compared to conventional propeller-driven planes. But there were many development problems concerned with jet-engine fuels, materials, and controls as well as with airplane design. The first turbojet airplane was the German Heinkel He 178 which flew in 1939. However, operational jets were a long time in coming.

THE Me 262

In 1942 the Germans began flying the Messerschmitt Me 262, the first operational jet fighter. It had devastating potential and could literally fly rings around all enemy aircraft. Moreover, it was heavily armed with four cannons and twenty-four rockets. However, the German hierarchy didn't realize what a potent plane they had and high production priority didn't come until 1945; much too late. Only a few hundred Me 262s saw combat, however these were very effective; a close call for the Allies.

MESSERSCHMITT Me 262 ATTACKING A B-17 FORMATION

THE F-86 SABRE

During the Korean conflict in the early 1950s two fighter aircraft emerged as natural rivals—the American F-86 Sabre and the Russian MiG-15.

The North American F-86 started as a 600-mile-per-hour fighter-design study near the end of World War II. As the technical lessons of the war were learned (including study of a captured German Me 262), the great advantage of swept-back wings and tail surfaces became apparent. These features allowed the plane to reach higher speeds without encountering the serious aerodynamic problems that slowed and disturbed the flight of conventional aircraft. To make the new swept-wing design manageable at low speeds, leading edge slats were added to the wings and the F-86 design was off to a successful start.

NORTH AMERICAN F-86 (BELOW) AND ITS NATURAL ENEMY THE SOVIET MiG-15 (ABOVE)

BOEING B-47 JET BOMBER TAKING OFF

THE B-47 STRATOJET

The Boeing B-47 was one of the United States' early jet-powered bombers, the first production version making its initial flight in 1950.

91

THE F-14 TOMCAT

A modern United States Navy all-weather jet fighter is the Grumman F-14 Tomcat. This plane is a twin-tailed brawler armed with many lethal airborne weapons, including the Phoenix interceptor missile. It flies faster than Mach 2, an engineering term meaning twice as fast as the speed of sound.

How do we achieve these high speeds, retain extreme maneuverability at moderate speeds, and still have adequate low-speed handling for landings on aircraft carriers? The designers of the Tomcat elected to use "swing wings." That is, the Tomcat's wings are pivoted so that they can be completely swept back for dash speeds, partially swept back for slower combat or in-flight refueling speeds, or left in the forward position for aircraft carrier launching and recovery.

THE SWING WING GRUMMAN F-14 TOMCAT (ABOVE); WING POSITIONS (BELOW)

GENERAL DYNAMICS F-16

THE LIGHTWEIGHT F-16

In 1972 the United States Air Force sponsored a competition to produce a comparatively inexpensive lightweight fighter that would be capable of speeds higher than Mach 2.

It had to be well-armed with cannon and missiles, and yet retain or improve upon the reliability and combat effectiveness of the existing heavier fighters (which weigh as much as 60,000 pounds). To achieve this, the manufacturers had to seek out and use advanced aero-

dynamic techniques, materials technology, and structural design. The result, in 1974, was the F-16 which weighed less than 30,000 pounds fully loaded and employed a highly advanced control system. It was a pilot's favorite from its first flights.

93

13. GENERAL AVIATION

MILITARY CURTISS JENNY

OX5 ENGINE

The term general aviation includes what is frequently called "private flying," "business flying," "sport flying," and "experimental aviation." It does not include commercial or military aviation.

THE JENNY

The Curtiss JN-4D known as the Curtiss Jenny, was designed to be the standard military trainer of World War I and it was mass produced. After the war, surplus Jennys were abundantly available and the army began to sell them, cheaply. The Jenny was generally powered by the Curtiss OX5, an engine that frequently broke down.

However, the Jenny brought aviation to all of America and was used by the flying barnstormer who would give airplane rides for about five dollars if he could manage to take off from the pasture in which he had recently landed.

BARNSTORMING IN A CURTISS JENNY

THE CUB

In 1930 C.G. Taylor designed the E-2 which became much better known as the Taylor Cub. The original Cub and its later versions became "everybody's trainer," an inexpensive two-passenger lightplane that flew well.

TAYLOR CUB

Over the years the Cub progressed from the improved J-2 model to the better J-3 and to more advanced models, while its manufacturers went through litigation, fires, and reorganizations. Finally William T. Piper emerged as the principal figure behind the Cub, and it became known as the Piper Cub. During World War II the Army bought thousands of the J-3 Cubs, naming its version the L-4 Grasshopper.

PIPER L-4 GRASSHOPPER

MODERN LIGHTPLANES

Shown here flying over a
small American town is a
Cessna Centurion. Planes
such as this serve the needs
of both business and pleas-
ure flyers.

CESSNA CENTURION

CZECHOSLOVAKIAN ZLIN AEROBATIC PLANE

THE AEROBATS

Aerobatic competitions resemble figure skating competitions in some ways. There are diagrammed standard maneuvers which must be flown precisely. In some events of a competition the combinations of maneuvers are known well in advance, in some they are divulged not long before the flight, and in some the combinations are up to the pilot. There have been many great aerobatic airplanes, but in the early 1970s the Pitts Special, flown by the United States Aerobatic Team, won practically every event.

Here we see a Pitts Special in the middle of a maneuver called a Lomcovak tumbling violently and surrounded by smoke that it generates for dramatic effect. The Lomcovak is one of many well known aerobatic maneuvers. Approved maneuvers must be flown with accuracy and crisp precision to win points at an aerobatic meet.

PITTS SPECIAL PERFORMING AN AEROBATIC ROUTINE

A less formal kind of aerobatics is sometimes called stunt flying, and it is frequently performed at air shows and at county and regional fairs. In this illustration we see a stunt pilot flying upside down in a modified Stearman Kaydet just after picking a ribbon off two poles with his vertical tail.

STUNT PILOT FLYING A STEARMAN KAYDET

BUSINESS AIRCRAFT

Business today requires easy and rapid transportation between cities and immediate seat availability for the business traveler. Many corporations have solved this problem by owning business airplanes and setting their own schedules.

There are many kinds of business planes. One of the most popular is the Learjet 25. This beautiful eight-passenger airplane owes its flashing performance to the fact that it was designed as an adaptation of a Swiss fighter concept.

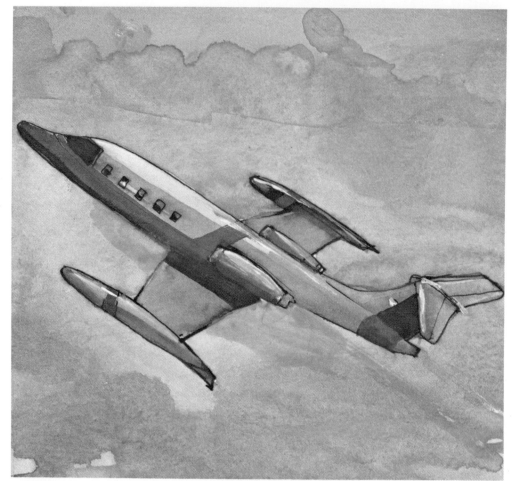

LEARJET 25

A newer variant of the Learjet, the ten-passenger Longhorn Model 56, features winglets, vertical surfaces at both wing tips. They were added to enable the wings to work more efficiently; to produce more lift with less drag.

LEARJET 56 LONGHORN

Parked at the general aviation terminal of a major airport we see the following business aircraft: from top to bottom, Saberliner 75A, Beechcraft C90, Beechcraft Bonanza V35B, and Cessna 2-10 Centurion.

SOME POPULAR BUSINESS PLANES

14. MODERN JET TRANSPORTATION AIRCRAFT

DE HAVILLAND COMET I

Although the first experimental jet plane flew in 1939, the world waited many years for the introduction of the first jet transport. During this period military jets were designed and built, but such designs could not meet the economy or safety goals for passenger airlines. However, by the late 1940s the design of a good jet transport finally seemed possible.

In the early 1950s de Havilland of Great Britain introduced the Comet, the world's first jet transport. But the Comet had a fatal design flaw, and some of the first Comets mysteriously began to fall from the sky after very few hours in service. The solution to this mystery is one of the great technological detective stories of our age.

An intensive study of the problem revealed that the metal in certain critical parts of the airplane could "fatigue" after a number of hours of normal operation. In metal fatigue repeated applications of stress can cause the metal to crack and the cracks spread (sometimes rapidly) until the structure breaks.

After much research a safe new structure was designed for the Comet and a new model called the Comet IV was put in service.

DE HAVILLAND COMET IV

BOEING 707

THE 707 AND DC-8

The maiden flight of the first Boeing 707, Model 367-80, usually referred to as the Dash 80, took place in 1954. From this beginning, the Boeing 707, in many different markings and versions, became the four-engined jet transport produced in the greatest quantity. Here we see a production model Boeing 707 flown by Pan American World Airways.

DOUGLAS DC-8 SERIES 61

The Douglas Aircraft Corporation, with its DC-8, was the second American manufacturer to develop a big, four-engined passenger jet. The DC-8 went into passenger service in late 1959 and became well known to seasoned travelers as the four-engined jet with the much bigger windows. Shown here is the DC-8, Series 61, an early jet transport with an ultra large passenger capacity, in some versions seating over 250 people.

THE ELECTRA

While Boeing and Douglas were designing and testing their all-jet transport airplanes, the 707 and DC-8, Lockheed Aircraft Corporation was producing the Electra, the only big American turboprop transport. The turboprop (sometimes called "propjet") engine develops most of its thrust by driving a conventional propeller with a gas turbine similar to the gas turbine in a turbojet engine.

Pilots loved to fly the Electra because it handled well, but the Electra's early life was marred by a peculiar and menacing puzzle. Two Electras had come apart in midair for no apparent reason. It was a designer's nightmare caused by a problem never before encountered in flight.

LOCKHEED ELECTRA

Investigation showed that somewhere in the engine installation a structural component had most probably broken, drastically lowering the stiffness of the engine housing or "nacelle." The result was a steadily increasing whirling and shaking of the engine and propeller during flight, so intense that in a short time it could cause a wing to break off.

Once this problem was studied and understood the plane's design was modified to prevent the catastrophic chain of events leading to this "propeller-whirl flutter" and the Electra had a productive service life.

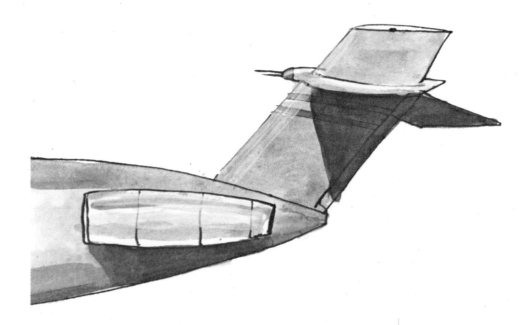

THE TWO-AND THREE-ENGINED *T* TAILERS

After the big long-haul four-engined turbojet transports were put in service, a new kind of jet transport was designed for shorter hauls. As the 707 was efficient on runs such as New York to Los Angeles, so the newer jets were good on runs like London to Paris.

Most of these new short-haul transports even looked different. The McDonnell Douglas DC-9 and the British Aircraft Corporation (BAC) One-Eleven are twin-engined examples. Note the two engines back near the tail.

BAC-ONE ELEVEN (ABOVE); McDONNELL DOUGLAS DC-9 (BELOW)

Others of the newer breed have three engines, two mounted on the fuselage near the tail and a third engine in the tail end of the fuselage. The Boeing 727 and Hawker Siddely Trident are examples of these. The appearance of all the airplanes mentioned here is similar in one respect: they all have *T* tails; that is the horizontal tail is mounted atop the vertical tail so that when seen from the rear the entire tail assembly resembles the letter *T*.

The proliferation of these *T* tailers in recent years has revolutionized business travel. It's now much easier to drive to the airport in the morning, fly to a city from 500 to 1500 miles away, transact business, and return home the same night.

BOEING 727 (ABOVE); HAWKER SIDDELY TRIDENT (BELOW)

THE WIDE-BODIED JETS

During the 1960s the increasing demand for air transportation led to a new kind of jet transport. Much bigger than the 707 and DC-8 types which seat up to 250 tourist-class passengers six-abreast, the new jets seat up to 350 eight-nine-or ten-abreast. These new big jet transports are generally known as "wide-body" jets.

An example of a wide-body jet is the Airbus A300, manufactured by a group of European companies in France, Germany, and Great Britain.

AIRBUS INDUSTRIES AIRBUS A300

109

Other examples are the American Boeing 747, McDonnell Douglas DC-10, and Lockheed L-1011. These wide-body jets and their successors seem destined to be the workhorses of the long-haul transport routes.

McDONNELL DOUGLAS DC-10 (TOP); BOEING 747 (CENTER); LOCKHEED L-1011 (BOTTOM)

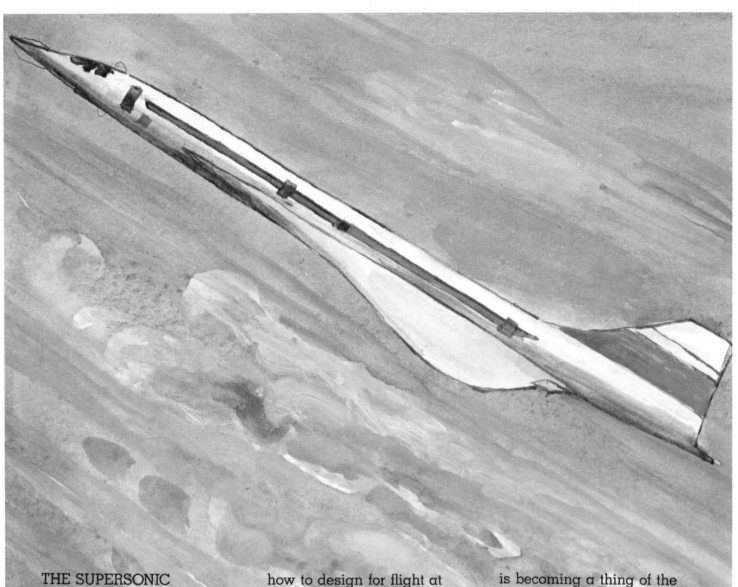

THE SUPERSONIC TRANSPORT

The modern all-jet transport airplanes described so far in this section typically fly at about 550 miles per hour. This is below the speed of sound in air. At speeds approaching or exceeding the speed of sound, aerodynamic and structural problems could develop and the planes might even fail catastrophically. This limitation on faster flight used to be known as the sound barrier, but actually, there is no such barrier—just a need to understand how to design for flight at higher speeds. Today's designers are trying to design transport airplanes that can fly efficiently at speeds as high as twice the speed of sound or faster—upwards of 1,300 miles per hour. Two types have been built. One is the Russian-produced Tupelov Model 144. The other is the Concorde supersonic transport, or SST produced by Aerospatiale of France and British Aircraft Corporation of Great Britain. Because of its high consumption of increasingly expensive fuel, the Concorde may be withdrawn from scheduled service. So as of the writing of this book, Supersonic passenger travel is becoming a thing of the past, not of the present, but perhaps it will also be a thing of the future. Engineering centers the world over are performing research in many areas which might lead toward more efficient flight and the development of alternative fuels. Success in some of these programs could lead to new and vastly improved SSTs. Until that day, time-conscious airline passengers will have to fly in subsonic jets which surpass all earlier planes in luxury and safety, and wait for what the future might bring.

AEROSPATIALE-BAC CONCORDE

SPACE SHUTTLE ORBITER *COLUMBIA*

CONCLUSION

We have summarized the progress of human flight from its vague beginnings in myths and legends to today's giant transports, powerful military aircraft, and convenient personal planes. What does the future hold?

Engineers, scientists, and business people are hard at work to make human flight better, safer, more affordable, and more useful. Will the time come when airplanes are used in place of automobiles? Will the time come when we can fly to other planets or to the stars? Who among us would have gone to the 1910 Belmont Park Air-meet and predicted that by 1960 many of us would be traveling in 707s? Similarly, who among us can foretell how flight will progress over the next fifty years? Manned flight is part of the great human adventure, and we will know about the future only when we get there.

GOSSAMER ALBATROSS

BIBLIOGRAPHY

The following books are among the many that were consulted in the preparation of this book and are also suggested for further reading on the subject. Because of the introductory nature of this book, this bibliography includes many picture books. Those that are out of print might be found in public library collections.

Giorgio Apostolo and Giorgio Begnozzi. *Color Profiles of World War I Combat Planes*. New York: Crescent Books, 1974.

Peter W. Brooks. *Historic Airships*. Greenwich, Connecticut: New York Graphic Society, 1973.

Heiner Emde. *Conquerors of the Air*. New York: Bonanza Books, 1968.

Thomas G. Foxworth. *The Speed Seekers*. New York: Doubleday & Company, 1976.

Charles Gibbs-Smith. *Aviation*. London, England: Her Majesty's Stationery Office, 1970.

Charles Gibbs-Smith. *Early Flying Machines*. London, England: Eyre Methuen, 1975.

Charles Gibbs-Smith. *Flight Through the Ages*. New York: Thomas Y. Crowell Company, 1974.

Charles Gibbs-Smith. *The Invention of the Airplane*. London, England: Faber and Faber, 1965.

William Green and Gordon Swanborough. *The Illustrated Encyclopedia of the World's Commercial Aircraft*. New York: Crescent Books, 1978.

Bill Gunston. *The Encyclopedia of the World's Combat Aircraft*. London, England: Salamander Books, 1976.

Peter Haining. *The Dream Machines*. New York: World Publishing, 1971.

Alvin M. Josephy, Jr. *The American Heritage History of Flight*. New York: American Heritage Publishing Company, 1962.

H.F. King, comp. *Milestones of the Air: Jane's 100 Significant Aircraft*. New York: McGraw Hill, 1979.

David Mondey, ed. *The Complete Illustrated Encyclopedia of the World's Aircraft*. New York: A & W Publishers, 1978.

David Mondey, ed. *The International Encyclopedia of Aviation*. New York: Crown Publishers, 1977.

Samuel Eliot Morison. *The Two-Ocean War*. Boston: Little, Brown and Company, 1963.

Henry R. Palmer, Jr. *Remarkable Flying Machines*. Seattle: Superior Publishing Company, 1972.

Gareth L. Pawlowski. *Flat-Tops and Fledglings*. New York: Castle Books, 1971.

The Romance of Ballooning. New York: The Viking Press, 1971.

Christopher Shores. *Fighter Aces*. London, England: Hamlyn, 1974.

John W.R. Taylor, ed. *Combat Aircraft of the World*. New York: G.P. Putnam's Sons, 1969.

John W.R. Taylor. *A History of Aerial Warfare*. London, England: Hamlyn, 1974.

John W.R. Taylor and Kenneth Munson, eds. *History of Aviation*. New York: Crown Publishers, 1972.

John W.R. Taylor, ed. *The Lore of Flight*. Gothenberg, Sweden: Tre Tryckare and Cagner & Company, 1970.

INDEX

HEATED-AIR SPORT BALLOONS

Melvin B. Zisfein is the Deputy Director of the National Air and Space Museum at the Smithsonian Institution in Washington, D.C. His interest in aeronautics dates back to his childhood in Philadelphia, Pennsylvania, where he was a member of "The Franklin Juniors," a club sponsored by the Franklin Institute for young people interested in science and technology. He attended the Massachusetts Institute of Technology and graduated with a Master of Science degree in Aeronautical Engineering. Since then he has worked with various aircraft companies as a designer and aerodynamicist and before going to the Smithsonian Institution was the Associate Director of Franklin Institute Research Laboratories in Philadelphia. He lives in Washington, D.C.

Robert Andrew Parker was born in Norfolk, Virginia and studied at the School of the Art Institute of Chicago. He is now widely known as a painter and printmaker, and his work is represented in collections around the world, including the Museum of Modern Art and the Whitney Museum of American Art in New York. He is also an award-winning illustrator of children's books, among them the 1970 Caldecott Honor Book, *Pop Corn and Ma Goodness*. He has been interested in flying since childhood and served in the Army Air Force as air crew in a B-25. He has five sons and lives in Connecticut.

MAY 1 3 1983			
DEC 1 8 1984			
OCT 2 7 1986			
APR 2 7 1988			
DEC 3 1992			
MAR 2 7 1995			
JAN 2 2 1998			
DEC 0 8 1998			

HIGHSMITH 45-108